Social Issues
in Literature

Women's Issues in Kate Chopin's *The Awakening*

Other Books in the Social Issues in Literature Series:

Social Issues in Literature

Women's Issues in Kate Chopin's *The Awakening*

Dedria Bryfonski, Book Editor

GREENHAVEN PRESS
A part of Gale, Cengage Learning

Detroit • New York • San Francisco • New Haven, Conn • Waterville, Maine • London

Elizabeth Des Chenes, *Managing Editor*

Articles in Greenhaven Press anthologies are often edited for length to meet page requirements. In addition, original titles of these works are changed to clearly present the main thesis and to explicitly indicate the author's opinion. Every effort is made to ensure that Greenhaven Press accurately reflects the original intent of the authors. Every effort has been made to trace the owners of copyrighted material.

Cover photograph courtesy of The Library of Congress.

LIBRARY OF CONGRESS CATALOGING-IN-PUBLICATION DATA

Women's issues in Kate Chopin's The awakening / Dedria Bryfonski, book editor.
    p. cm. -- (Social issues in literature)
  Includes bibliographical references and index.
    ISBN 978-0-7377-5819-1 (hardcover : alk. paper) -- ISBN 978-0-7377-5820-7 (pbk. : alk. paper)
  1. Chopin, Kate, 1850-1904. Awakening. 2. Chopin, Kate, 1850-1904--Political and social views. 3. Women in literature. 4. Sex roles in literature. 5. Suicide in literature. 6. Upper class women--United States--Social conditions. I. Bryfonski, Dedria.
  PS1294.C63A6438 2011
  813'.4--dc22
                                  2011017998

Printed in the United States of America
2 3 4 5 6   18 17 16 15 14

Contents

Chapter 2: *The Awakening* and Women's Issues

Chapter 3: Contemporary Perspectives on Women's Issues

Introduction

Every now and then a book comes along that differs radically from all the books that came before it, a book that pushes the boundaries of literary convention. *Nineteen Eighty-Four* by George Orwell belongs to this category, as does D.H. Lawrence's *Lady Chatterley's Lover* and Gustave Flaubert's *Madame Bovary*. *The Awakening*, published in 1899, is also generally considered to be such a trailblazing novel. Many critics consider it to be the first artistically successful novel written by an American woman. In *The Awakening*, Kate Chopin shattered the stereotypical view of respectable womanhood with her portrayal of a woman who desired both personal and sexual freedom. Although sexually active women had been depicted previously in European fiction, American writers had rarely acknowledged a woman's sexuality, unless as an example of a general moral failing. And, as has been the case with many groundbreaking novels, *The Awakening* shocked its contemporary audience and needed to wait many years before it could be appreciated for the masterpiece it is.

What was the genesis of this novel? How did a genteel, upper-class nineteenth-century southern woman come to create such a revolutionary novel? The roots of artistic genius can never be unequivocally explained. The circumstances of Kate Chopin's life and the era in which she wrote, however, encouraged independence and open-mindedness. Her education and family members stimulated her creativity, and her study of European writers gave her examples of artistry and a Continental sensibility.

The period around the turn of the twentieth century was one that saw a significant change in the role of women, to the extent that the phrase "New Woman" was coined to set apart this new creature from her predecessors. Prior to this time, a woman's role was seen exclusively in the home, as mother, wife, and keeper of the house. With the dawn of the Industrial Revolution, jobs became available outside the home, and many lower-class women found a new freedom that comes from financial independence. In 1870 barely 1 percent of women worked outside the home in clerical positions; that number had increased to more than 25 percent by 1920. Women from the middle and upper classes were becoming better educated. By 1920 females accounted for 55 percent of all high school students and 60 percent of all high school graduates. Southern women were among those changing. In *The Reconstruction of White Southern Womanhood, 1865–1895*, Jane Turner Censer argues that due to the Civil War, "the ideal womanhood, along with traditional values of self-sacrifice and duty, had come to include a more active, outspoken, and courageous aspect." Certainly, the war reduced the fortunes of many southern families and forced many women to become more independent. Censer's research found that the generation of women born between 1850 and 1869 were the most accepting of change. Kate Chopin was born in 1850, on the cusp of this generation of southern women who were more questioning of their traditions.

In 1848 the country's first women's political convention was held in Seneca Falls, New York, headed by Lucretia Coffin Mott and Elizabeth Cady Stanton. The Seneca Falls convention called for women to be granted the right to vote and set the groundwork for the women's rights movement. Over the coming years, the nascent feminist movement would spread in a variety of ways. For upper-class women, one of the avenues was through the establishment of women's clubs. These clubs were formed to give women a place to discuss political and social issues and to further the cause of women's rights. Additionally, many women's clubs began tackling some of the social issues of the day by providing support and education for poor women.

Thus Chopin was born into an era that was beginning to embrace change and, especially, to question the traditional role of women. Chopin's own family history contributed to her streak of independence and flouting of conventions. She was only five years old when her father died, and she was raised by three strong women—her great-grandmother, grandmother, and mother. From them she learned independence and resilience, characteristics that helped her meet the challenges that life had in store for her. She was only thirty-five years old when her husband died, leaving her with six children and significant debts. Due to some bad business decisions made by her husband, she needed to economize and to develop additional sources of income to maintain her family. Thus Chopin moved back to St. Louis to live with her mother and turned to writing at the encouragement of her obstetrician and friend, Dr. Frederick Kolbenheyer. Among the independent women Chopin was exposed to, it was perhaps her unconventional great-grandmother who exerted the strongest influence. From her great-grandmother, young Kate was introduced to the art of storytelling and to unconventional ideas. According to critic Helen Taylor in *Gender, Race, and Region in the Writings of Grace King, Ruth McEnery Stuart, and Kate Chopin*, Chopin, who was born Kate O'Flaherty,

> came from a family of early French settlers, many of them free-thinkers and rebels against legal, sexual, and racial conventions. There had been divorce, adultery, and some miscegenation in her mother's side of the family. . . . Kate O'Flaherty's great-grandmother, generally acknowledged to have been a raconteuse and a strong influence on the young girl, had legally separated parents, and herself married in 1797 when three months pregnant. She enjoyed telling her great-granddaughter tales of the early city's founder Pierre Laclede's adultery with his lieutenant's mother, Madame Chouteau. Stories such as this are said to have inspired Kate with the knowledge of unorthodox, daring women, providing subjects for her fiction. The many examples of her own

immediate family and her ancestors can thus be seen as offering role models and possible subjects for her later work.

Biographers are aware of numerous instances when Chopin came in contact with the developing feminist movement. Perhaps the most significant was on her honeymoon when she met noted feminist Victoria Claflin Woodhull on a train to New York. In her diary, Chopin noted that the suffragist was a "fussy, pretty, talkative little woman" who "entreated me not to fall into the useless degrading life of most married ladies, but to elevate my mind and turn my attention to politics, commerce, questions of state, etc. I assured her I would do so."

On her return to St. Louis following the death of her husband, Chopin became actively involved in the social and intellectual life of this cosmopolitan city. For a time she was part of a women's club that pressed for the advancement and education of poor women. More significantly, she became a leading member of the literary colony of the city and established regular open houses on Thursday where people—mostly men—met to talk about books and ideas. In an interview for a PBS (Public Broadcasting Service) show on his grandmother, Chopin's grandson David Chopin remembers:

> It was really a kind of byway, an inn or hotel for just about every artistic person who came through town and was in town. She used to have these Thursday afternoon soirees and all the poets and the writers and the editors and people who happened to be in town were there. She sat there like the Grand Dame she was and entertained them.

Chopin's unconventional upbringing had fostered a creative, independent, and exceptional woman. Kolbenheyer, one of the leading intellectuals of St. Louis, would expand her horizons by introducing her to the works of authors and thinkers whose influence would add depth and complexity to her writings. Charles Darwin, Thomas Huxley, Émile Zola, Gustave Flaubert, Guy de Maupassant, and Walt Whitman were some of the writers Chopin began reading at the suggestion of her friend. The Europeans, in particular Maupassant, inspired Chopin with their psychological realism, use of imagery, and Continental approach to sexuality and women's issues.

Chopin would go beyond her models, however, to create in *The Awakening* the story of a sensual woman who was unrepentant about her sexuality and her desire for independence. Worse, in her critics' eyes, was that Chopin evidently felt sympathy for her "immoral" character. Most reviews of *The Awakening* were harsh. Chopin suffered socially as a result, and the book soon went out of print.

In writing about the unconventional life of her central character, Edna Pontellier, Chopin was in some respects anticipating her own career as a writer. According to critic Elaine Showalter in "Tradition and the Female Talent: *The Awakening* as a Solitary Book":

> The parallels between the experiences of Edna Pontellier, as she breaks away from the conventional feminine roles of wife and mother, and Kate Chopin, as she breaks away from conventions of literary domesticity, suggest that Edna's story may also be read as a parable of Chopin's literary awakening. Both the author and the heroine seem to be oscillating between two worlds, caught between contradictory definitions of femininity and creativity, and seeking either to synthesize them or to go beyond them to an emancipated womanhood and an emancipated fiction. Edna Pontellier's "unfocused yearning" for an autonomous life is akin to Kate Chopin's yearning to write works that go beyond female plots and feminine endings.

Chronology

1850

Katherine O'Flaherty (Kate Chopin) is born on February 8 to Thomas O'Flaherty, an Irish immigrant, and Eliza Faris, a Creole.

1855

Kate Chopin begins school at the Academy of the Sacred Heart in St. Louis. In November her father dies in a rail accident. Following the accident, she leaves school to study at home with her great-grandmother.

1863

Kate's great-grandmother Victoire Verdon Charleville dies on January 16, and her half-brother, George, a Confederate soldier, dies of typhoid fever on February 17.

1865

Kate returns to the Academy of the Sacred Heart.

1868

Kate graduates from the Academy of the Sacred Heart.

1870

Kate marries Oscar Chopin on June 9 in St. Louis. In October they move to Chopin's native New Orleans.

1871

The Chopins' first child, Jean Baptiste, is born on May 22 in New Orleans.

1873

The Chopins' second child, Oscar Charles Chopin Jr., is born in St. Louis on September 24. On December 27 Kate's brother Thomas is killed in an accident in St. Louis.

1874

The Chopins move to the Garden District of New Orleans. The Chopins' third child, George Francis, is born in St. Louis on October 28.

1876

The Chopins' fourth child, Frederick, is born in New Orleans on January 26.

1878

The Chopins' fifth child, Felix Andrew, is born in New Orleans on January 8.

1879

Oscar's cotton business fails, and the Chopins move to Cloutierville, Louisiana. The Chopins' only daughter, Lelia, is born in Cloutierville on December 31.

1882

Oscar dies of malaria on December 10.

1884

Kate Chopin moves with her children back to St. Louis.

1885

Chopin's mother dies on June 28.

1888

Chopin writes her first poem, "If It Might Be," and begins the story "Euphrasie."

1890

Chopin's first novel, *At Fault*, is published privately in September. She becomes a charter member of the Wednesday Club.

1894

Bayou Folk is published on March 24.

1897

Chopin's grandmother Athènaïse Charleville Faris dies on January 27. *A Night in Acadie* is published in November.

1899

The Awakening is published on April 22 and receives mostly negative reviews.

1904

Chopin attends the St. Louis World's Fair, where she has a stroke on August 20. She dies on August 22.

Social Issues
in Literature

CHAPTER 1

Background on
Kate Chopin

The Life of Kate Chopin

Sara deSaussure Davis

Sara deSaussure Davis is associate professor emeritus of English at the University of Alabama. She has authored and edited several works on American literature, including The Mythologizing of Mark Twain *and* Kate Chopin Reconsidered: Beyond the Bayou.

Although Kate Chopin's frank exploration of a woman's sexuality in The Awakening *scandalized the literary establishment of her era, the passage of time has led to the realization that the novel is a masterpiece, Sara deSaussure Davis contends in the following viewpoint. Throughout her career, Davis asserts, Chopin was concerned with the conflict between the individual and society and also the role of women in society. In* The Awakening, *she explores the powerlessness of women in the Victorian age, held hostage, in Davis's view, by their marriages and children.*

Kate Chopin introduced to the reading public a new fictional setting: the charming, somewhat isolated region along the Cane River in north central Louisiana, an area populated by Creoles, Acadians, and blacks. Beginning in the 1960s, her fiction was also recognized for its new psychological terrain, especially in her depiction of women who experience the power of passion that often brings them into conflict with society. Instead of comparing Chopin to the Louisiana local colorists—George Washington Cable, Ruth McEnery Stuart, or Grace King; or even to Mary E. Wilkins Freeman and Sarah Orne Jewett, the local colorists of New England—critics now compare her exploration of new themes to the innovations of

Sara deSaussure Davis, "Katherine Chopin," *Dictionary of Literary Biography, American Realists and Naturalists*, Donald Pizer and Earl N. Harbert, eds. Belmont, CA: Gale Research, 1982, pp. 59–71. Copyright © 1982 by The Gale Group. Reproduced by permission.

other daring writers of the 1890s: Stephen Crane, Hamlin Garland, and Frank Norris. It is true that her first published novel, *At Fault* (1890) and her two published collections of short fiction, *Bayou Folk* (1894) and *A Night in Acadie* (1897), are set in or refer to the Cane River area and convincingly portray the distinctive customs, language, and atmosphere of the region. The popularity in her own time of such local-colorist qualities, combined with the condemnation of her frank depiction of female sexuality in *The Awakening* (1899) have somewhat obscured Chopin's other achievements. Literary historians of the first half of [the twentieth] century perpetuated some important misjudgments or misinformation about her fiction and her career, typically praising her as the author of "Désirée's Baby" (a short story about, among other things, the tragic effects of miscegenation) while seldom mentioning *The Awakening*, now considered her masterpiece. On occasion the plot of the short story has been attributed to the novel. A corrective to the stale second- or thirdhand assessments of her work came in 1946, when the French critic Cyrille Arnavon called attention to Chopin's place in the realistic tradition of France and America. Although she treats in *The Awakening* what are basically naturalistic ideas of heredity and environment, the essence of her work remains best described as realistic. Since Arnavon's work, a Chopin revival has taken place, in part stimulated by the work of another European scholar, Per Seyersted, who wrote the definitive biography and edited *The Complete Works of Kate Chopin* (1969).

Chopin Dealt with Loss Early in Her Life

Most of the important experiences that shaped Kate Chopin's temperament and subject matter occurred in the first thirty-three years of her life, before she began to write professionally. Born in St. Louis [Missouri] to secure and socially prominent parents, Eliza Faris O'Flaherty, of French-Creole descent, and Thomas O'Flaherty, an Irish immigrant and successful commission merchant, Katherine O'Flaherty attended the St. Louis Academy of the Sacred Heart; she graduated in 1868 and par-

Kate Chopin (1851–1904), author of The Awakening *(1899).* The Library of Congress.

ticipated in the social life of a belle for two years before she married a Creole, Oscar Chopin of Louisiana, in June 1870.

Kate O'Flaherty's great-grandmother, Mme. Victoria Verdon Charleville, lived in the O'Flaherty household and directed young Kate's mental and artistic growth until her death when Kate was eleven. She cultivated in the young girl a taste for storytelling, a relish for the intimate details about such historical figures as the earliest settlers of the Louisiana Territory, and an unabashed, unhesitant, even unjudgmental intellectual curiosity about life. Additionally, she superintended the girl's piano lessons and her French, the language especially important in their bilingual home. Chopin's interest in music was lifelong, as was her willingness to explore unconventional ideas. The young Kate was known in St. Louis as the town's "Littlest Rebel" for having taken down and hidden a Union flag from her home where "the Yanks tied it up." A Unionist neighbor managed to keep her from being arrested, but the severity of her offense may be judged by the fact that in New Orleans a man was shot for the same violation.

During her childhood, Kate Chopin endured the death of her father, as well as several other family deaths. Although she always recovered, the depth of her grief may be sensed by her reaction as an eleven-year-old to the deaths (that occurred within a month) of both Mme. Charleville and her half brother George, who fought on the Confederate side during the Civil War. For about two years Chopin withdrew from school, from friends, even somewhat from her family, and spent much of the time reading in the attic. Yet in her fiction—"Ma'ame Pélagie," for example—as in her life, she stressed the moral and psychological value of living in the present.

In 1869, before she had met her future husband, she met a German woman in New Orleans who combined fame as a singer and actress with a respectable place in society and a wealthy, loving husband. This meeting exhilarated the recently graduated Kate Chopin. She also began smoking during this trip, a pleasure she indulged [in] with relish and humor all her life.

Chopin's Influences

Kate and Oscar Chopin lived for almost a decade in New Orleans, until his cotton factoring business failed in 1879, whereupon they moved to Cloutierville, Natchitoches Parish, in north central Louisiana. In both New Orleans and in Cloutierville she absorbed impressions that she would later employ in her fiction. The combination of her gift as a mimic with her talent as a musician—she played by note and by ear and had a remarkable memory for music—allowed her to capture the distinctive cadences, nuances, gestures, and diction of the residents of Louisiana who would, years later, people her fiction. She was at home in New Orleans and Cloutierville society, partly because of her personal magnetism but also because of her faultless French and her Southern sympathies.

In the fertile cotton land around the Cane River, the Chopins lived on inherited property, with income from the management of several small plantations and the ownership of a plantation store. Although they were not living on a plantation themselves, they were intimately involved in the festive plantation society. By 1879, Kate Chopin had borne her sixth child and only daughter, and by 1883 she was a widow, her husband dead of swamp fever. For a year she successfully managed his business duties, but in 1884 returned with her family to St. Louis, to live with her mother. Her mother's death followed shortly afterward in 1885, leaving Chopin without family—except for her six children—and with a small, diminishing income.

Her only close friend during this time was Dr. Frederick Kolbenheyer, her mother's neighbor and her own obstetrician for three of her children, a learned man whose encouragement is believed to have led her to study contemporary science, to give up her religious beliefs, and to start writing professionally. Following a visit to Natchitoches in 1887, she wrote a poem, "If it might be," published 10 January 1888 in *America*, a progressive Chicago magazine; this publication marked her first appearance in print. She also began working on two pieces of fiction, one titled "Euphrasie," which was much later revised and published as "A No Account Creole" in *Century* (1894), and one she referred to in a notebook as "An

Unfinished Story—Grand Isle—30,000 words," which she later destroyed. In an unpublished draft of an essay written in 1896, she describes herself as she struggled initially to shape her personal self into a fictive one and credits [popular French short story writer] Guy de Maupassant with helping her find a vision as well as technique and theme: "It was at this period of my emerging from the vast solitude in which I had been making my own acquaintance, that I stumbled upon Maupassant. . . . Here was a man who had escaped from tradition and authority, who had entered into himself and looked out upon life through his own being and with his own eyes." She particularly responded to his spontaneity and his ability to create genuine impressions "without the plots, the old fashioned mechanism and stage trapping that in a vague, unthinking way I had fancied were essential to the art of story making."

Her first two stories to reach print, "Wiser than a God" and "A Point at Issue!" were written and published in 1889; both concern the unconventional attitude of the heroine toward marriage as a reflection of her unconventional attitude toward herself. This subject would become a persistent but not single-minded theme in Chopin's work, culminating in *The Awakening* as well as in the unpublished short story "Charlie," written in 1900. She came to the theme naturally, not ideologically, partly at least through the strong influence of her great-grandmother, Mme. Charleville. . . .

Early Works Depict a Louisiana Milieu

Chopin's first novel, *At Fault*, was written after "Euphrasie," the first draft of "A No Account Creole." These works are the first to employ the region, families, concerns, and ambiance of Natchitoches Parish. Written between July 1889 and April 1890, *At Fault* presents the intertwined questions of divorce and moral idealism and announces a number of Chopin's future themes: the relation of the individual to change and to society, the problems of romantic love and unrestrained passion, and the dilemma of the modern woman. . . .

Contemporary reviews of *At Fault* praised its author's characterizations, style, and humor, while complaining about its breaches of respectability in diction and action. By and large, *At Fault* was seen as a promising first novel. Now, the novel's refusal to condemn divorce is recognized as a first in fiction, and Chopin's willingness to describe a female alcoholic is also a departure from conventional expectations.

In 1890 Chopin worked primarily on her second novel, *Young Dr. Gosse*, which was finished in January 1891 and sent to several publishers but was never accepted. She then returned to shorter fiction, completing about forty pieces in the next three years. Twenty-three of these stories, four previously unpublished, were collected in *Bayou Folk*, published by Houghton, Mifflin in March 1894. By then, Chopin had broken out of the local St. Louis periodicals and children's magazines that first published her work and into the eastern literary market, though the subject matter of several of the stories caused delays as she searched for more tolerant forums. In 1894 her stories appeared in *Century, Atlantic,* and *Vogue. Vogue*, in fact, published nineteen of her stories from 1893 to 1900, among them her most provocative and outspoken on the themes of a woman's sexual nature and her situation in marriage, including "Désiree's Baby," "La Belle Zoraïde," "A Respectable Woman," "The Story of an Hour," "The Kiss," "Her Letters," "An Egyptian Cigarette," and "The White Eagle."

Bayou Folk depicts more fully the Louisiana milieu of *At Fault*. The tales are unified by setting, recurring characters, a prevailing theme, and the author's tone—cool and distant but with humor and insight. The setting is occasionally New Orleans but predominately Natchitoches Parish, whether the village of Natchitoches, the plantations along Cane River, the small farms and squalid cabins, or the houses on the bayous. Chopin reveals herself here as a practitioner of Howellsian realism [in the style of American author and critic William

Dean Howells]—portraying ordinary people in their everyday concerns. Except for two stories set during the Civil War, the tales take place after the war, the effects of which are apparent in the narratives. The war indirectly provides the main plot in four of the twenty-three stories, but in each the family at home supplies the angle of vision.

The major theme of the *Bayou Folk* collection is love, whether loyal devotion, romantic love, love of honor, sexual passion, or some combination of these. Love is a positive force for the individuals involved and for their community. Devotion to another takes many forms. Yet even devotion has complexity when examined from Chopin's ironic perspective. For example, in "A Lady of Bayou St. John" a childlike wife whose husband is fighting with [Confederate general P.G.T.] Beauregard falls in love with a neighboring Frenchman and plans to flee to Paris with him. But before she does, word comes that her husband is dead. Instead of marrying the Frenchman she devotes herself to the memory of her husband. Is devotion to an ideal more satisfying than love itself, and is a dead husband more capable of inspiring fidelity than a living one, or has the passion she experienced with the Frenchman enabled her, ironically, to sacrifice as well as to love? Chopin leaves the enigma unresolved. . . .

Chopin Begins Writing *The Awakening*

The success of *Bayou Folk* no doubt contributed to Chopin's continuing to write short stories. She was not receiving much encouragement for her still unpublished second novel, *Young Dr. Gosse*; in 1895 it was rejected again, and in 1896 she destroyed it. Her working methods and living conditions probably also influenced her to write shorter fiction. Valuing spontaneity in art as in life, she often composed a story in one sitting and most of her stories were printed as they were first written. She said of her own writing, "I am completely at the mercy of unconscious selection. To such an extent is this true, that what is called the polishing up process has always proved disastrous to my work, and I avoid it, preferring the integrity of crudities to artificialities." Chopin worked in the living room, subject to the demands of her family. Her children remember her sitting in their midst with a lapboard and writing materials, refusing to exclude them, even though she wished to at times. The youngest of her six children was eighteen when Chopin began her next novel, *The Awakening*. Throughout her career, she wrote only one or two days a week, leaving the rest of the time for such activities as musicales [evenings of home musical entertainment], concerts, and the theater. She also presided over the equivalent of a French salon, which attracted St. Louisians of various intellectual interests.

Chopin's second collection of tales, *A Night in Acadie*, which came out in 1897, contains twenty-one stories, all but one of which had first been published in a periodical. Way and Williams, the book's Chicago publisher, was not well known, and this work received less notice than *Bayou Folk*. The milieu and some of the characters are the same as in *Bayou Folk*, but the themes of this second volume are more diverse. The number of stories about devotion falls to two. In place of charmingly depicted romantic love is a more complicated sexual passion. The demands of passion, the reconciliation of public with private self, and the resurrection from a static life are interrelated themes in this collection and point toward Chopin's next book and finest achievement, *The Awakening*. Fifteen tales are equally divided among these three topics; three of the remaining four are miscellaneous sketches, brief insights into character. . . .

Chopin Addresses Erotic Themes

The few reviews *A Night in Acadie* attracted praised Chopin as a local colorist but reacted against the book's sensual themes. The collection is now praised both for its success in the local-color genre and for its indication of Chopin's maturing artistry.

From 1897 to 1900 or 1901, Chopin tried unsuccessfully to market a third collection of stories, called "A Vocation and a Voice." It contained in its final version twenty-one stories, one written before 1894, sixteen written between 1894 and 1897, and four written after 1897. About half of the stories had been published in *Vogue*, a number had been difficult to place because of their subject matter, and five were not to see print until many years after Chopin's death. *Vogue* was clearly aware that Chopin's themes were often daring, and its editors gave her her most consistently tolerant forum.

The variation of themes begun in *A Night in Acadie* increases in this collection, and Chopin moves away from her usual Louisiana setting. Moreover, the characters and themes establish themselves authentically without the Louisiana dialect or setting (present in only three tales), and for the first time Chopin experiments effectively in several pieces with first-person narration. Among these stories are three brief sketches that concern nature as a means of knowledge, specifically a knowledge of God. The remaining tales are almost equally divided: about half deal frankly with the imperatives of passion; the rest can be grouped together not so much by theme as by their most salient quality—an ironic tone, closest in spirit perhaps to [novelist] Stephen Crane's irony.

Many of the stories treat extramarital sex as a subject of interest for what it reveals of human psychology, not as a subject of lament or moralizing, anticipating Chopin's handling of the theme in *The Awakening*. Furthermore, in the title story, "A Vocation and a Voice," as well as in "Lilacs," "Two Portraits," and "Juanita," she suggests in a [Walt] Whitmanesque fashion that to obey erotic impulses is to participate in the natural rhythms of life itself. . . .

In addition to some forty poems and several translations (including seven of Maupassant's tales), Chopin also wrote and had published a small number of essays, among them literary reviews. With the exception of one piece that appeared in the *Atlantic Monthly*, most of the essays were published in St. Louis journals from 1894 to 1897. Not surprisingly, she proves as a critic to be consistent with her own practice of art. For example, in two 1894 essays she chastises [novelist] Hamlin Garland for dismissing "from the artist's consideration such primitive passions as love, hate, etc.," and she criticizes [French novelist Émile] Zola's method in "Lourdes" because the story is "more than two-thirds of the time swamped beneath a mass of prosaic data, offensive and nauseous description and rampant sentimentality." While her criticism was often acute, Chopin's major achievement remains her fiction, particularly *The Awakening*.

The Awakening Creates a Scandal

Now often republished and acclaimed as a masterpiece, *The Awakening* was during Chopin's lifetime the subject of scandal and censure. Certain contemporary reviews of the novel depicted the moral and literary biases of her critics, who termed the book "moral poison," "sordid," "unhealthy," "repellent," and "vulgar" with "disagreeable glimpses of sensuality." Accusing Chopin of "out Zola-ing Zola," reviewers were offended because the author did not condemn her adulterous heroine, Edna Pontellier, or, worse, that she seemed at times to sympathize with Edna. In spite of the moral outrage it engendered, the novel also drew some reluctant praise for its artistry and insight. Typical was the comment of her friend, writer C.L. Deyo: "It is sad, and mad and bad; but it is all consummate art." Libraries in St. Louis banned the book, and acquaintances and even some friends cut [off] Chopin socially. In fact, reactions to the novel were later credited with paralyzing Chopin's creativity.

The vehemence of the hostile reviews of *The Awakening*, which assuredly contributed to its half century of neglect, is attributable to the novel's special power. That power derives not so much from Chopin's violation of several nineteenth-century principles of womanly and literary decorum, although that violation raised indignant protests, as from the novel's intense poetic unity: the prose style, the characterization of the heroine, and the symbolism all lead inevitably to the novel's tragic resolution. Indeed, Chopin's contemporary reviewers often seem to protest loudest against their own sympathy with Edna.

The poetic beauty of *The Awakening* derives from its organic unity of symbolism and plot, traceable in part to Chopin's methods of composition and in part to Chopin's mature mastery of form and theme. Just as she tended to write a short story in a burst of concentrated writing, Chopin worked on *The Awakening* from about mid-1897 until 21 January 1898, during which time she probably wrote only one other work, the short story "A Family Affair"; thus she gave the novel her full creative effort. The manuscript was submitted to Way and Williams but when they went out of business, they transferred it in November 1898 to Herbert S. Stone and Company, and the novel was published 22 April 1899. According to the author's notebooks, *The Awakening* earned $145 between 1899 and 1901.

The Awakening was in many ways—despite all the 1890s' celebration of the New Woman—a novel ahead of its time. . . .

The Theme of Women's Lack of Control

Two crucial scenes—the delivery of Adèle's child and Edna's suicide—dramatize the novel's major themes. Through the description of the delivery and the subsequent conversation between the physician and Edna, Chopin expresses the idea that children (and by implication, marriage) control the lives of women because of the imperatives of biology as well as of society. . . .

Edna's idealized love for Robert sustains her in the face of her disillusionment, but after she finds him gone, she seems to believe it inevitable that she will never find such compensation again. After a long night's meditation, she journeys to Grand Isle, where the only embrace and comfort she finds are those promised by Death as both lover and self-realization. An evocative, musical refrain that recurs throughout the book has foreshadowed this paradoxical symbolism of the waters at Grand Isle. . . .

The original title of the novel, *The Solitary Soul,* points to the essential, radical aloneness of Edna, whose transcendent self is only realized in death, a "defeat," as [linguist] Donald Ringe says, "that involves no surrender." Chopin's sympathies were no doubt engaged by Edna's tragic dilemma, yet she refrains from all moralizing about Edna's suicide, content to examine with courage and honesty without reaching for easy moral judgments.

The treatment of eros in *The Awakening* has rightly been compared to Greek tragedy, to Whitman's poetry, and to D.H. Lawrence's novels, while in its analysis of a woman's role in marriage and society, the novel bears a strong though not derivative resemblance to both [Gustave Flaubert's] *Madame Bovary* and [Henry James's] *The Portrait of a Lady.* The public outcry stirred by *The Awakening* makes it comparable to [Theodore Dreiser's novel] *Sister Carrie,* published in 1901; Chopin, like Dreiser, was unwilling to compromise her artistic vision.

The effect of the unfavorable reviews for *The Awakening* was compounded in 1900 by another rejection of Chopin's third collection of stories, as well as by the return of her piece "Ti Démon" from the *Atlantic,* which termed the story "too sombre." Nevertheless, she did not completely cease writing as a result of these disappointments, as has been popularly maintained. She wrote some nine stories after April 1899, three of which were published before her death. . . .

The Relationship of Self and Society

Although she had not been in good health since 1903, and had not written anything since then, Kate Chopin became an enthusiastic daily visitor to the 1904 St. Louis World's Fair.

Following one day at the fair she suffered a cerebral hemorrhage and died two days later, on 22 August 1904.

Lacking a good editor who might have provided encouragement or simply good editing for her sometimes artless diction, Kate Chopin did not accomplish what she might have during a career shortened by her death. Nevertheless, she is distinguished for the frankness with which she approached sexuality, the amorality with which she described such problems as divorce and adultery, and for the serious consideration she gave to the restrictions of marriage and childbearing and the uses of freedom. Freed from conventional American male viewpoints by an inheritance that came naturally to Chopin— her French culture and her female perspective—possessed of a graceful wit and an intelligent honesty, Kate Chopin spoke of woman's condition in American society in a way that her contemporaries could not or would not. But she also, in both male and female characters, explored that persistent American concern, the relationship between self and society.

The Controversy over *The Awakening* Wounded Chopin

Felix Chopin

Felix Chopin was one of Kate Chopin's five sons.

In the following viewpoint, the youngest of her five sons writes a personal reminiscence of his mother. Felix Chopin reveals that his mother was more comfortable in the short story genre, writing novels at the insistence of her editors. She was deeply distressed by the negative reaction to The Awakening, *claims Felix. Although Kate Chopin was an accomplished and beautiful woman, her son writes that she led a simple life and was by nature a loner.*

She was always a great reader, and was particularly fond of [French short story writer Guy] de Maupassant. However, she had done no writing until persuaded by Dr. Fred Kolbenberger *sic*], a friend of hers, who was deeply impressed by the letters she had written him while away from St. Louis on a trip.

Chopin Was Primarily a Short Story Writer

Dr. Kolbenberger was often a guest in the home, a man of great learning, who would speak for hours on the life and career of Napoleon [Bonaparte].

One evening Mother had a curious psychic experience. She went to the Olympic Theatre with a friend to see a play, and in the middle of the performance, suddenly got up and said, "I must go home at once—something has happened to [Chopin's daughter] Lelia." A carriage was called; they hurried

Felix Chopin, "Statement on Kate Chopin," *A Kate Chopin Miscellany*, Per Seyersted, ed. Natchitoches, LA: Northwestern State University of Louisiana, 1979, pp. 166–68. Copyright © 1979 by Northwestern State University of Louisiana. Reproduced by permission.

to her home, and found Lelia in bed, sleeping peacefully. However, at the time she was in the Theatre, Lelia had almost been critically burned by a spark from the grate fire catching on her garments. She had had the presence of mind to wrap herself in a rug and put it out.

Mother was essentially a short story writer, but her editors became insistent that she write a novel. "I never thought her first one [At Fault] was any good." Her second novel [The Awakening], however, created a furor which hurt her deeply. In it, a woman permits a man to kiss her on the neck. Many newspapers and libraries treated the book as indecent. The Mercantile Library, among others, took it out of circulation, and Mother resigned her membership as a result. She was broken hearted at the reaction to the book.

Mother always sought comfort—physical comfort. As a young woman she had learned to smoke cigarettes in Louisiana where many women smoked at that time. Got Cuban cigarettes.

Our living room was very comfortable. Grate fire. She had a sort of day bed made by carpenters, wider than modern daybeds, and with deep cushions.

She wrote sitting in a Morris Chair [an early recliner], on a board resting on the arms of the chair. There, sitting beside the grate, she would write intensely, and very rapidly. Often there were long periods between her stories, but when she started writing, she wrote very fast, and on completion, seldom had to make more than a few slight corrections.

She loved to play cards, particularly whist.

Chopin Was Not an Active Feminist

She was not interested in the woman's suffrage movement. But she belonged to a liberal, almost pink-red [i.e., leftist] group of intellectuals, people who believed in intellectual freedom and often expressed their independence by wearing eccentric clothing.

Among her circle of friends was [author and editor] William Schuyler [and] William (?) Blackman.

These friends would meet for informal Sunday evening suppers—al fresco in the summertime.

She was a great admirer of William Marion Reedy [editor of *Reedy's Mirror*].

She never made very much from her writings. Her short stories were published in the *Youth's Companion, Century Magazine*, etc.

She belonged to the Wednesday Club.

She was in many ways, a lone wolf.

She was beautiful as a girl, about five feet, five inches tall, with grayish-brown eyes, a low, well modulated voice. Her hair turned gray when she was young, and was becoming. Later she became stout but even then was a handsome woman.

She was fond of music, and played the piano. She organized with her friends, musicales [evenings of musical entertainment].

The Awakening Was Misunderstood and Criticized

Emily Toth

Emily Toth is a professor of English at Louisiana State University. The author or editor of numerous books on Kate Chopin and a coeditor of Kate Chopin's Private Papers, *Toth is considered one of the most influential biographers and critics on the Louisiana author.*

Both earlier and modern-day readers of The Awakening *have difficulty understanding the subtleties of the novel, claims Emily Toth in this selection. Early critics found the heroine unsympathetic and the plot unwholesome, she explains. Contemporary readers are often confused by the sexual descriptions, which, in Toth's view, needed to be veiled to be publishable in the late 1800s.*

A century after the novel first appeared, teachers of *The Awakening* often ask their students to summarize the plot—and no two ever come up with the same story. Kate Chopin's 1899 novel is complex and subtle, and readers can argue endlessly about which scenes and features and characters are most important. They also wonder about the ending: is it positive? is it negative? is it over? (Novelist Jill McCorkle has suggested that Edna is still out there swimming, bent on finding a good time to come back.) Many modern readers wonder whether they are supposed to like Edna, understand her, or loathe everything about her.

The Awakening Confuses Critics

Most of Kate Chopin's original critics had little trouble with any of those questions.

Emily Toth, *"The Awakening," Unveiling Kate Chopin.* Jackson: University Press of Mississippi, 1999, pp. 209, 211–17, 219–21, 224–27. Copyright © 1999 by University Press of Mississippi. Reproduced by permission.

According to the majority of 1899 reviews, *The Awakening*'s Edna Pontellier is a selfish wife and mother who not only does not appreciate her good husband, but she also rebels in the worst possible way—by taking a lover or two. She is not sympathetic; she is wicked, foolish, or both. As for the ending, the journal *Literature* expressed the common view of 1899: "the waters of the gulf close appropriately over one who has drifted from all right moorings, and has not the grace to repent."

That was not the way Kate Chopin saw her novel. Asked to describe it, she might have said something about the imagery—the birds, the water—and about the settings: the natural wonders of Grand Isle, the urban bustle of New Orleans....

A century later, in fact, some parts of the plot are hazy to literal-minded readers.

Confusing Descriptions of Sexuality

Sex is a major barrier. Modern readers expect more graphic language, and are prone to misunderstand the intimacies they do see. There is, for instance, *The Awakening*'s chapter VII, in which Edna and Madame Adèle Ratignolle, both handsome women who enjoy each other's company, go down to the beach together at Grand Isle. That summer, Edna has been startled by the Creole "absence of prudery," and especially by Adèle's comforting, caressing touches. Readers a century later, confusing sexuality and sensuality, sometimes see more than what is there—and think there is a "lesbian" connection between the two.

There is indeed, if "lesbian" means love between women, or what Chopin calls, in that chapter, "the subtle bond which we call sympathy, which we might as well call love." But the word "lesbian" was not in common use in Chopin's day: women who loved women were not put in a separate category under a different label. In the 1890s Edna and Adèle are, in Chopin's terms, "intimate friends." That does not mean what it would mean, bluntly, a century later—a genital connection. It does mean a unique and sometimes wordless emotional and spiritual understanding, the kind that unlocks Edna's thoughts about herself.

There are other things in *The Awakening* that are still to be unlocked—such as the sexual orientation of Robert, Edna's summer cavalier. He is definitely different from the other fellows. They all smoke cigars, manly and phallic; Robert smokes cigarettes, as women do (he claims they're cheaper). The other men hold jobs in the city, while Robert hangs about with his mother and attaches himself to a different unattainable—usually married—woman every summer. Clean-shaven and light-haired, he resembles Edna, and the husbands regard him as a safe puppy dog. But Adèle Ratignolle, more discerning, asks Robert to leave her friend Edna alone. Edna is an outsider: "She is not one of us; she is not like us. She might make the unfortunate blunder of taking you seriously."

When Robert objects that he is not a clown or a jack-in-the-box, Adèle gives an even stronger hint about what he really is: "If your attentions to any married women here were ever offered with any intention of being convincing, you would not be the gentleman we all know you to be, and you would be unfit to associate with the wives and daughters of the people who trust you."

Not long after that, and without consulting Edna, Robert flees to Mexico.

Before he leaves, though, Robert encounters Mr. Pontellier in the city, and Edna wonders if he seemed "gay." Her husband says Robert was cheerful, which is "natural in a young man about to seek his fortune and adventure in a strange, queer country."

When Robert returns, he has a pouch embroidered by—he says—a girl in Vera Cruz. But homosexual male Americans frequently went to Mexico for sexual alliances with boys ("Vera Cruz" is an easy pun on cruising). Robert may very well love

Edna, but when she grabs him aggressively in their last scene together, her gesture tells him that he will have to perform sexually, as a man with a woman. And so (at least according to modern queer readings), if Robert is a gay man, recognizable to other Creoles as gay, he has to run away.

If readers a century ago interpreted Robert as homosexual, no one said so in print, just four years after [British playwright] Oscar Wilde's sensational trial for homosexuality. Possibly the codes for recognizing a gay male character were well known to avant-garde readers in 1899, and they had no need to write down what they already knew.

Meanwhile, our language for recognizing heterosexuality has also shifted. In Kate Chopin's day, readers of *The Awakening* knew exactly what Edna was doing with Alcée Arobin, but a century later, they are less sure. They wonder, for instance, which body parts are involved—but Chopin could not have named the sexual parts of her characters and gotten her book published. She and her contemporaries used literary conventions, just as filmmakers once used symbolic images—fires flaming up, waves crashing across the sand—as shorthand for sexual acts they could not show. (In the movie version of *Gone with the Wind*, sex is understood to take place between the time Rhett carries Scarlett up the stairs and the next morning, when she awakens in bed.)

Kate Chopin's contemporaries would recognize that, in *The Awakening*, Edna has sexual relations with Alcée Arobin on three separate occasions, all indicated by suggestive language and white space. A century later, high school teachers, embarrassed by students' questions and doubtful themselves about literary conventions, often deny that Edna and Arobin actually "do it." They do, and in these chapters: (1) At the end of XXVII: "It was the first kiss of her life to which her nature had really responded. It was a flaming torch that kindled desire." In the white space after that passage, the sex takes place, followed by:

XXVIII

Edna cried a little that night after Arobin left her. (2) At the end of XXXI: "He did not answer, except to continue to caress her. He did not say good night until she had become supple to his gentle, seductive entreaties." (3) In XXXV: After a night drive with his fast, unmanageable horses, Arobin and Edna arrive at her little house "comparatively early in the evening."

It was late when he left her. It was getting to be more than a passing whim with Arobin to see her and be with her. He had detected the latent sensuality, which unfolded under his delicate sense of her nature's requirements like a torpid, torrid, sensitive blossom.

That passage can also be read as clitoral imagery, but Chopin's contemporary readers—if they thought so—could never have said so in print.

Kate Chopin got her ideas, she said, from "the spontaneous expression of impressions gathered goodness knows where. To seek the source, the impulse of a story is like tearing a flower to pieces for wantonness." Still, bits of her life undeniably feed into the settings and characters of *The Awakening*, and at least some of her "impressions" can be traced to Impressionism. ("Impressions" is also the title of her 1894 diary.)

Chopin Borrowed from Her Experiences

Chopin knew what it was like to be an outsider in Louisiana: she never lost that feeling. She had been a great walker around New Orleans; she had summered in the tropical paradise in Grand Isle. She had heard, all her life, the secrets women told each other when no men were around. And she drew on some of her own secrets, and some of other people's. . . .

Many bits from Kate Chopin's life feed into *The Awakening*.

The characters' names, for instance, come from different layers of her past. In her New Orleans years, she learned from

A paperback edition of The Awakening *published in 1999, one hundred years after its original publication.* Time & Life Pictures/Getty Images.

[artist] Edgar Degas about his friend Berthe Morisot and her sister Edma, the painter who gave up her art when she married Adolphe Pontillon in 1869, a year before the Chopins arrived in New Orleans. (Edma Morisot Pontillon regretted that sacrifice for the rest of her life.) Degas's New Orleans neighbor Léonce Olivier, meanwhile, was the impeccable but uninteresting husband whose wife left him for another man some years later. And so Kate Chopin combined the names: Edma Pontillon, the artist silenced by marriage, and Léonce Olivier, the unsatisfactory husband, easily became Edna and Léonce Pontellier.

Degas obviously shared other gossip, too, a quarter-century before Kate Chopin used it in *The Awakening*. Besides her sister, Berthe Morisot had one other very close friend, a beautiful blonde sculptor and exceptional confidante who called herself "Marcello"—but her real name was Adèle Colonna. Hence the first name Adèle for Edna Pontellier's blonde, beautiful confidante. Adèle's last name, Ratignolle, recalls an 1870 painting that Degas knew well: "The Batignolles Studio," a very large group portrait of major contemporary artists, painted by Henri Fantin-Latour. (It may also be from Fantin-Latour that Chopin chose the pen name "La Tour" for her two pseudonymous stories, "The Falling in Love of Fedora" and "Miss McEnders.")

As for Edna's other friend Mademoiselle Reisz: she has no first name, and Chopin gives no clue as to how her name should be pronounced. But according to her friend Will Schuyler, Chopin did read the French novelist Alphonse Daudet, who in 1878 published a novel called *Le Nabab*, about a woman artist who believes herself to be monstrously different, because she defies the rules of traditional society. . . .

The artist heroine's name is Félicia Ruys—an unpronounceable name.

From her Cloutierville years, Kate Chopin chose the names of Edna's lovers, giving each one part of *Albert* Sampite's[1] first

---

1. Allegedly, Kate Chopin and Albert Sampite had an affair after her husband's death.

name: *Al-*cée and Ro-*bert*. Arobin also resembles Sampite as a figure of great temptation: dark, reckless, sexual, arrogant. For *The Awakening*, Chopin brought together her lifelong observation of women's dreams and desires and her knowledge of French literature, where some of those emotions could be portrayed openly. . . .

There were plenty of other inspirations from real life. Her brother-in-law Phanor Breazeale, for instance, told Chopin about a French Quarter woman who had desires that marriage could not fulfill—while [editor] Billy Reedy published a similar story in the *Mirror*, about a married woman from St. Louis who became enmeshed in a painful summer romance. She was "a fine figure of a woman" but "somewhat addicted to sentimentality"—which made her vulnerable to "a young Baltimorean with good looks and a taste for poetry" and "romantic professions." She hung about him in public; she claimed he was the only one who could teach her to swim. Some letters were sent, the young man's father came to take his son away, and the husband was overheard furiously saying "something about 'puppy-love letters' and an 'asylum.'" When the lady returned to St. Louis, Reedy predicted, "she will be surprised to find how much news of her season has preceded her."

For Sophisticated Readers Only

When *The Awakening* appeared, less than two years later, that story may have been another reason for the "best people" of St. Louis to resent Kate Chopin. . . .

The Awakening is the unveiling of Edna Pontellier, and the first prepublication reviewer—a woman—recognized that. [Lucy Monroe] called it, in *Book News* for March 1899, "a remarkable novel," keen and subtle, "an intimate thing, which in studying the nature of one woman reveals something which brings her in touch with all women—something larger than herself." Kate Chopin "pictures, too, with extraordinary vividness, the kind of silent sympathy which is sometimes the expression of the love that goes deep." *The Awakening* shows "a brilliant kind of art." . . .

After Monroe's, there were some favorable small notices. The *St. Louis Republic*, in March, called *The Awakening* the story of an "intensely real" woman who "finally awakens to the fact that she has never lived." *The Book Buyer*, in April, called the book "analytical and fine-spun, and of peculiar interest to women."

Those were among the last good notices *The Awakening* received. . . .

[After that,] *The Awakening* was . . . pummeled by reviewer after reviewer. Reedy assigned the book to Frances Porcher, a critic and short story writer who objected to anything that strayed from "the ideal." To Porcher, Edna's character was "sensual and devilish," and "One would fain beg the gods, in pure cowardice, for sleep unending rather than to know what an ugly, cruel, loathsome monster Passion can be when, like a tiger, it slowly stretches its graceful length and yawns and finally awakens." Porcher praised Chopin's skill as a writer, but "it leaves one sick of human nature and so one feels—*cui bono* [who benefits]?"

Chopin had to expect a negative review from the St. Louis *Globe-Democrat*, still owned by Ellen McKee ("Miss McEnders"), and she got it. The *Globe-Democrat* praised the book's local color, but termed it "not a healthy book; if it points any particular moral or teaches any lesson, the fact is not apparent."

But as if waiting in the wings, Chopin's friend Charles L. Deyo flew out to defend *The Awakening* in the *Post-Dispatch*. His review criticizes Léonce Pontellier for treating his wife as "a bit of decorative furniture," and calls Edna, fairly, "not good enough for heaven, not wicked enough for hell." Deyo praised Chopin's "subtle understanding of motive," and said a story like Edna's calls for "compassion, not pity." No doubt abetted by discussions at Chopin's "Thursdays," Deyo also attacked the genteel insistence on bland and innocent stories and readers. "*The Awakening*, is not for the young person," Deyo declared, though "not because the young person would be harmed by reading it, but because the young person wouldn't understand it." It is a book, he said, for "seasoned souls, for those who have ripened under the gracious or ungracious sun of experience." It also was not for

> the old person who has no relish for unpleasant truths. For such there is much that is very improper in it, not to say positively unseemly. A fact, no matter how essential, which we have all agreed shall not be acknowledged, is as good as no fact at all. And it is disturbing—even indelicate—to mention it as something which, perhaps, does play an important part in the life behind the mask.

> It is sad and mad and bad, but it is all consummate art. . . .

In short, *The Awakening* was an honest and fearless book that could be understood only by smart and sophisticated people— like those Deyo and Chopin knew best.

Chopin Was Supported by Friends

Meanwhile, Chopin's friends did not think it was too late to form a loyal circle around her. When the *Globe-Democrat* published its vicious review, the attorney Lewis Ely—one of her many younger male admirers—sent a note suggesting to Chopin: "Provide yourself with ammonia salts, brandy, etc. You have had or will have hysterics, I'm sure. I didn't know there was such a fool in the world as the writer of that article."

Chopin's women friends, at least the more literary ones, also condemned the critics. Anna L. Moss, a clubwoman and sometime book reviewer, wrote to Chopin that the reviews showed "on the whole, as much discrimination as one could expect from such sources." To Moss, *The Awakening* was delicate, charming, true to life and much too good for the reviewing public: "it is not surprising that but few of the reviewers are more than funny."

Other friends chimed in. A friend signed "L." praised Chopin's "emancipation of the whole being from the trammels of conventionalism," and quoted a Mr. Paul who called Chopin "an undoubted genius."

A Louisville friend, who signed her note Lizzie L., called the book "faultless," with delicious humor, and added "In many places I can hear you speaking, describing incidents in your own cute, inimitable way." As an extra cheering-up treat, Lizzie L. enclosed gossip about a mutual friend.

But over the summer of 1899, *The Awakening* was being buffeted by mostly bad reviews from coast to coast. Chopin stayed at home even during the muggiest days of August and stubbornly kept her salon going. She needed the comfort of friends, and—as always—she attracted the admiration of younger men. . . .

Meanwhile, Kate Chopin's faith in her own literary career was taking a beating. On November 8, she wrote a Utah correspondent that she had had "a severe spell of illness" and was "only now looking about and gathering up the scattered threads of a rather monotonous existence." The illness may well have been depression: she did seem to be hiding from people. . . .

Libraries Did Not Ban *The Awakening*

Whatever buzzings there may have been, Kate Chopin was not ostracized in St. Louis. Her *Post-Dispatch* friends in late November devoted almost an entire page to "A St. Louis Woman Who Has Won Fame in Literature," and the Wednesday Club rallied to honor her with one of its largest and best-attended gatherings.

The *Post-Dispatch* shrewdly positioned Kate Chopin as a Southern lady, with a drawing of her first home—made to look like a Southern mansion with galleries and columns. The article also included "Mrs. Chopin's Workroom From a Water Color Sketch By Her Son, Oscar Chopin": a well-appointed room with bookcases on either side of the fireplace, a musical clock, a nude Venus, and—in an armchair—Kate Chopin herself, leaning back and looking ethereal. The article praised Kate Chopin as a "universal" writer, "not sectional or provincial," with an appeal to "the finer taste. . . . Her art is not a cunning composition, but a living thing." Chopin also contributed an essay about her walking and writing habits—claiming, as always, to be un-serious and spontaneous.

A certain asperity crept in, though, when she wrote: "How hard it is for one's acquaintances and friends to realize that one's books are to be taken seriously, and that they are subject to the same laws which govern the existence of others' books!" Many an acquaintance had nagged her son with questions about where to get his mother's book. Chopin herself grew tired of telling people, politely, to try the booksellers or the libraries.

"The libraries! Oh, no, they don't keep it," a friend might claim, and "She hadn't thought of the bookseller's. It's real hard to think of everything! Sometimes I feel as if I should like to get a good, remunerative job to do the thinking for some people."

That comment about the libraries helped create a myth, generations later, that *The Awakening* had been banned and withdrawn from libraries—but it hadn't. The Mercantile Library and the St. Louis Public Library both bought multiple copies and kept them on the shelves until they wore out, as late as 1914 for the last one. Americans do like stories of banned books, but Billy Reedy—who loved to fulminate about censorship—would have gone into a volcanic rage if such a thing had happened to his friend Kate Chopin.

Chopin Was Influenced by Strong Women

Bernard Koloski

Bernard Koloski is professor emeritus of English at Mansfield University in Pennsylvania. He has written extensively about Kate Chopin and is the author of Kate Chopin: A Study of the Short Fiction.

There were several influences in Chopin's early life that would show up later in her fiction, Bernard Koloski suggests in the following excerpt. She was mentored by strong women—her grandmother, her mother, the Sacred Heart nuns, and her friend Kitty Garasché. Of French heritage, Chopin was bilingual and French literature and culture were influences in her writing, Koloski explains. She became an author following the untimely death of her husband and enjoyed early success as a short story writer. However, Koloski asserts, the frank sexuality of her second novel, The Awakening, *scandalized reviewers of the time. It would take critics writing after the 1950s to recognize the artistry of her work.*

American author Kate Chopin (1850–1904) wrote two published novels and about a hundred short stories in the 1890s. Most of her fiction is set in Louisiana and most of her best-known work focuses on the lives of sensitive, intelligent women.

Chopin's Reputation Revived in the 1950s

Her short stories were well received in her own time and were published by some of America's most prestigious magazines—*Vogue,* the *Atlantic Monthly, Harper's Young People, Youth's*

Companion and the *Century*. A few stories were syndicated by the American Press Association. Her stories appeared also in her two published collections, *Bayou Folk* (1894) and *A Night in Acadie* (1897), both of which received good reviews from critics across the country. About a third of her stories are children's stories—those published in or submitted to children's magazines or those similar in subject or theme to those that were. By the late 1890s Kate Chopin was well known among American readers of magazine fiction.

Her early novel *At Fault* (1890) had not been much noticed by the public, but *The Awakening* (1899) was widely condemned. Critics called it morbid, vulgar, and disagreeable. Willa Cather, who would become a well known twentieth-century American author, labeled it trite and sordid.

Some modern scholars have written that the novel was banned at Chopin's hometown library in St. Louis, but this claim has not been able to be verified, although in 1902, the Evanston, Illinois, Public Library removed *The Awakening* from its open shelves. Chopin's third collection of stories, to have been called *A Vocation and a Voice*, was for unknown reasons cancelled by the publisher and did not appear as a separate volume until 1991.

Chopin's novels were mostly forgotten after her death in 1904, but in the 1920s her short stories began to appear in anthologies, and slowly people again came to read her. In the 1930s a Chopin biography appeared which spoke well of her short fiction but dismissed *The Awakening* as unfortunate. However, by the 1950s scholars and others recognized that the novel is an insightful and moving work of fiction. Such readers set in motion a Kate Chopin revival, one of the more remarkable literary revivals in the United States.

After 1969, when [literary scholar and writer] Per Seyersted's biography, one sympathetic to *The Awakening*, was published, along with Seyersted's edition of her complete works, Kate Chopin became known throughout the world. She has attracted great attention from scholars and students, and her work has been translated into other languages, including Dutch, Portuguese, Czech, Korean, Polish, German, Spanish, and Japanese. She is today understood as a classic writer who speaks eloquently to contemporary concerns. *The Awakening*, "The Storm," "The Story of an Hour," "Désirée's Baby," "A Pair of Silk Stockings," "A Respectable Woman," "Athénaïse," and other stories appear in countless editions and are embraced by people for their sensitive, graceful, poetic depictions of women's lives.

Chopin's Early Life Was Eventful

Catherine (Kate) O'Flaherty was born in St. Louis, Missouri, USA, on February 8, 1850, the second child of Thomas O'Flaherty of County Galway, Ireland, and Eliza Faris of St. Louis. Kate's family on her mother's side was of French extraction, and Kate grew up speaking both French and English. She was bilingual and bicultural—feeling at home in different communities with quite different values—and the influence of French life and literature on her thinking is noticeable throughout her fiction.

From 1855 to 1868 Kate attended the St. Louis Academy of the Sacred Heart, with one year at the Academy of the Visitation. As a girl, she was mentored by women—by her mother, her grandmother, and her great grandmother, as well as by the Sacred Heart nuns. Kate formed deep bonds with her family members, with the sisters who taught her at school, and with her life-long friend Kitty Garasché. Much of the fiction Kate wrote as an adult draws on the nurturing she received from women as she was growing up.

Her early life had a great deal of trauma. In 1855, her father was killed in a railroad accident. In 1863 her beloved French-speaking great grandmother died. Kate spent the Civil War in St. Louis, a city where residents supported both the Union and the Confederacy and where her family had slaves in the house. Her half brother enlisted in the Confederate army, was captured by Union forces, and died of typhoid fever.

From 1867 to 1870 Kate kept a "commonplace book" in which she recorded diary entries and copied passages of essays, poems, and other writings. In 1869 she wrote a little sketch, "Emancipation: A Life Fable."

At eighteen, Kate was an "Irish Beauty," her friend Kitty later said, with "a droll gift of mimicry" and a passion for music. At about nineteen, through social events held at Oakland, a wealthy estate near St. Louis, Kate met Oscar Chopin of Natchitoches Parish, Louisiana, whose French father had taken the family to Europe during the Civil War. "I am going to be married," Kate confided in her commonplace book, "married to the right man. It does not seem strange as I had thought it would—I feel perfectly calm, perfectly collected. And how surprised everyone was, for I had kept it so secret!" Kate and Oscar were married in 1870.

On their wedding trip the couple traveled to Cincinnati, Philadelphia, and New York, and then crossed the Atlantic and toured Germany, Switzerland, and France. They saw Paris only briefly, in September, 1870, during the Franco-Prussian War, at a moment when the city was preparing for a long siege. Kate never visited Europe again.

Music and Culture in New Orleans

Back in the States, the couple settled in New Orleans, where Oscar established a business as a cotton factor, dealing with cotton and other commodities (corn, sugar, and molasses, among them). Louisiana was in the midst of Reconstruction at the time, and the city was beset with economic and racial troubles. Oscar joined the notorious White League, a Democratic group that in 1874 had a violent confrontation with Republican Radicals, causing President [Ulysses S.] Grant to send in federal troops.

But New Orleans also offered superb music at the French Opera House, along with fine theatre, horse races, and, of course, Mardi Gras. Kate may have met the French painter Edgar Degas, who lived in New Orleans for several months around 1872. She would have been observing life in the city, gathering material that she could draw upon for her fiction later in life. Like other wealthy families in the city, the Chopins would go by boat to vacation on Grand Isle, a Creole resort in the Gulf of Mexico.

Between 1871 and 1879 she gave birth to five sons and a daughter—in order of birth, Jean Baptiste, Oscar Charles, George Francis, Frederick, Felix Andrew, and Lélia (baptized Marie Laïza).

In 1879 the Chopins moved to Cloutierville, a small French village in Natchitoches Parish, in northwestern Louisiana, after Oscar closed his New Orleans business because of hard financial times.

Oscar bought a general store in Cloutierville, but in 1882 he died of malaria—and Kate became a widow at age thirty-two, with the responsibility of raising six children. She never remarried.

In 1883 and 1884, Chopin's recent biographer, Emily Toth, has written, Kate had an affair with a local planter. But she then moved with her family back to St. Louis where she found better schools for her children and a richer cultural life for herself. Shortly after, in 1885, her mother died.

As a mature adult, Barbara Ewell writes, Kate "was a remarkable, charming person. Not very tall, inclined to be plump, and quite pretty, she had thick, wavy brown hair that grayed prematurely, and direct, sparking brown eyes. Her friends remembered most her quiet manner and quick Irish wit, embellished with a gift for mimicry. A gracious, easygoing hostess, she enjoyed laughter, music, and dancing, but especially intellectual talk, and she could express her own considered opinions with surprising directness."

Begins Writing After Becoming a Widow

Dr. Frederick Kolbenheyer, her obstetrician and a family friend, encouraged her to write. Influenced by [French short story writer] Guy de Maupassant and other writers, French and American, Kate began to compose fiction, and in 1889 one of her stories appeared in the *St. Louis Post Dispatch*. In 1890 her first novel, *At Fault*, was published privately. The book is about a thirtyish Catholic widow in love with a divorced man. Like Edna Pontellier in *The Awakening*, Thérèse Lafirme struggles to reconcile her "outward existence" with her "inward life." She cannot as a practicing Catholic accept the idea of divorce, yet she cannot banish from her life the man whom she loves. *At Fault* offers a compelling glimpse into what Kate Chopin was thinking about as she began her writing career.

Chopin completed a second novel, to have been called *Young Dr. Gosse and Théo*, but her attempt to find a publisher failed and she later destroyed the manuscript. She became active in St. Louis literary and cultural circles, discussing the works of many writers, including Georg Wilhelm Friedrich Hegel, Émile Zola, and George Sand (she had called her daughter Lélia, apparently after the title of Sand's 1833 novel).

During the next decade, although maintaining an active social life, she plunged into her work and kept accurate records of when she wrote her hundred or so short stories, which magazines she submitted them to, when they were accepted (or rejected) and published, and how much she was paid for them:

In 1889 she wrote "A Point at Issue!" and in 1891 rewrote "A No-Account Creole" (which she had originally written in 1888) and wrote the children's story "Beyond the Bayou" and other stories. Five of her stories appeared in regional and national magazines, including *Youth's Companion* and *Harper's Young People*.

She wrote "Désirée's Baby" and the little sketch "Ripe Figs" in 1892. "At the 'Cadian Ball" appeared in *Two Tales* that year, and eight of her other stories were published. The next year she wrote "Madame Célestin's Divorce," and thirteen of her stories were published. Chopin traveled to New York and Boston to seek a publisher for a novel and a collection of stories.

In 1894 she wrote "Lilacs" and "Her Letters." "The Story of an Hour" and "A Respectable Woman" appeared in *Vogue*. And Houghton Mifflin published *Bayou Folk*, a collection of twenty-three of Chopin's stories.

Success as a Writer

Bayou Folk was a success. Chopin wrote that she had seen a hundred press notices about it. The collection was written up in the *New York Times* and the *Atlantic*, among other places, and most reviewers found its stories pleasant and charming. They liked its use of local dialects.

Chopin traveled that year to a conference of the Western Association of Writers in Indiana and published in *Critic* an essay about her experience, an essay that offers a rare insight into what she thinks about writers and writing. "Among these people," she says, "are to be found an earnestness in the acquirement and dissemination of book-learning, a clinging to the past and conventional standards, an almost Creolean sensitiveness to criticism and a singular ignorance of, or disregard for, the value of the highest art forms."

"There is," she continues, "a very, very big world lying not wholly in northern Indiana, nor does it lie at the antipodes, either. It is human existence in its subtle, complex, true meaning, stripped of the veil with which ethical and conventional standards have draped it."

Also in 1894 Chopin published in *St. Louis Life* a review of *Lourdes* by the French writer Émile Zola. She did not much like the book, but the way she begins her review is illuminating:

I once heard a devotee of impressionism admit, in looking at a picture by [painter Claude] Monet, that, while he himself had never seen in nature the peculiar yellows and reds therein depicted, he was convinced that Monet had painted them because he saw them and because they were true. With something of a kindred faith in the sincerity of Mons. Zola's work, I am yet not at all times ready to admit its truth, which is only equivalent to saying that our points of view differ, that truth rests upon a shifting basis and is apt to be kaleidoscopic.

Her 1894 comment about the importance of describing "human existence in its subtle, complex, true meaning, stripped of the veil with which ethical and conventional standards have draped it" and her conviction that "truth rests upon a shifting basis and is apt to be kaleidoscopic" are helpful points of reference in approaching Kate Chopin's work.

In 1895 Chopin wrote "Athénaïse" and "Fedora," and twelve of her stories were published. In 1896 she wrote "A Pair of Silk Stockings." "Athénaïse" was published in the *Atlantic Monthly.* In 1897 Way and Williams (of Chicago) published *A Night in Acadie,* a collection of twenty-one Chopin stories.

Like *Bayou Folk,* her earlier collection, *A Night in Acadie* was praised by the critics. One reviewer called it "a string of little jewels," and a modern critic considers it one of America's great nineteenth-century books of short stories.

Chopin's grandmother, Athénaïse Charleville Faris, died in 1897. Chopin worked on *The Awakening* that year, finishing the novel in 1898. She also wrote her short story "The Storm" in 1898, but, apparently because of its sexual content, she did not send it out to publishers. Probably no mainstream American publisher would have printed the story. The next year, 1899, one of her stories appeared in the *Saturday Evening Post,* and Herbert S. Stone published *The Awakening.*

Mostly Negative Reviews

A few critics praised the novel's artistry, but most were very negative, calling the book "morbid," "unpleasant," "unhealthy," "sordid," "poison." . . .

Two of Chopin's stories were published in *Vogue* in 1900. Herbert S. Stone, for unknown reasons, canceled her contract for *A Vocation and a Voice*, a third collection of her stories (the collection was published by Penguin Classics in 1991). In 1902 "A Vocation and a Voice," the title story of Chopin's proposed volume, was published in the *St. Louis Mirror*. Her last published story appeared in *Youth's Companion*.

In 1904 Kate Chopin bought a season ticket for the famous St. Louis World's Fair, which was located not far from her home. It had been hot in the city all that summer, and Saturday, August 20, was especially hot, so when Chopin returned home from the fair, she was very tired. She called her son at midnight complaining of a pain in her head. Doctors thought that she had had a cerebral hemorrhage.

She lapsed into unconsciousness the next day and died on August 22. She is buried in Calvary Cemetary in St. Louis, where many people visit her gravesite and sometimes leave behind tokens of their affection.

It took half a century for people to grasp what Kate Chopin had accomplished with her work. In his introduction to a paperback edition of *The Awakening* in 1964, Kenneth Eble speaks of Chopin's "underground imagination"—"the imaginative life which seems to have gone on from early childhood somewhat beneath and apart from her well-regulated actual existence."

George Arms a few years later writes that in her work Kate Chopin "presents a series of events in which the truth is present, but with a philosophical pragmatism she is unwilling to extract a final truth. Rather, she sees truth as constantly reforming itself and as so much a part of the context of what happens that it can never be final or for that matter abstractly stated."

And in his 1969 biography, Per Seyersted argues that Chopin "broke new ground in American literature."

"She was," Seyersted continues, "the first woman writer in her country to accept passion as a legitimate subject for serious, outspoken fiction. Revolting against tradition and authority; with a daring which we can hardly fathom today; with an uncompromising honesty and no trace of sensationalism, she undertook to give the unsparing truth about woman's submerged life. She was something of a pioneer in the amoral treatment of sexuality, of divorce, and of woman's urge for an existential authenticity. She is in many respects a modern writer, particularly in her awareness of the complexities of truth and the complications of freedom."

Since 1969, countless scholars have written about Chopin's life and work. Feminist critics have had an enormous influence. Most of what has been written about Kate Chopin since 1969 is feminist in nature or is focused on women's positions in society. Sandra Gilbert's introduction to the Penguin Classics Edition of *The Awakening*, for example, and Margo Culley's selection of essays for the Norton Critical Edition of the novel are familiar to a generation of readers, although scholars have also been dealing with other subjects and themes. . . .

Today Kate Chopin is widely accepted as one of America's essential authors.

Social Issues
in Literature

CHAPTER 2

The Awakening and Women's Issues

An Appreciation of Art Symbolizes an Awakening to Independence

Miriam J. Shillingsburg

Miriam J. Shillingsburg is dean of the College of Liberal Arts and Sciences at Indiana University, South Bend.

In The Awakening, *Edna chooses a life that questions rather than accepts society's values. This choice is brave but doomed, according to Miriam J. Shillingsburg in the following viewpoint, because Victorian society was not accepting of a truly independent woman. In Shillingsburg's view, Edna's path to personal independence is symbolized by her growing appreciation of art and music. Women of this era were able to exercise some control over their surroundings through their art, but this control did not extend to their personal lives, Shillingsburg contends.*

Feminists and others have recently discovered Edna in Kate Chopin's astounding novel, *The Awakening*, published in 1899. It is the story, on the obvious level, of a young wife's awakening to sexual love outside her marriage. But at deeper levels it is the awakening of the self of Edna Pontellier in conflict with the culture, symbolized in part by Edna's stirring appreciation of music and by her fledgling attempts to paint.

Edna Is at Odds with Society

Chopin's biographers agree that she had had a happy marriage with six children when her husband died in Kate's thirty-second year, in 1883. About five years later she began to write

Miriam J. Shillingsburg, "The Ascent of Woman, Southern Style: Hentz, King, Chopin," *Southern Literature in Transition: Heritage and Promise*, Philip Castille and William Osborne, eds. Memphis, TN: Memphis State University Press, 1983, pp. 136–39. Copyright © 1983 by Memphis State University Press. Reproduced by permission.

"hesitatingly," and her earliest work is known mainly for its local color characteristics. Many of her works center on a strong, determined young woman, often a wife, who rebels against husband and society; but the endings of these stories are varied so as not to put forward a single solution for the "place" of women. One of the protagonists runs away from home only to return at the discovery of her impending motherhood; another only wants to spend some money frivolously; one converts from tomboy to feminine mystique.

However, with Edna, Chopin wrote what seems today a thoroughly honest account of a woman at odds with her society's values. This central figure is . . . an upper-class woman, the wife of a highly respected Creole businessman Léonce Pontellier. Because she is by upbringing a Presbyterian, Edna is unused to the customs of the less introspective, more free-wheeling Creole wives who spend their summers on Grand Isle. When Robert Lebrun flirts with them, they warn him that Edna "might make the unfortunate blunder of taking [him] seriously." And soon Robert and Edna appear to be in love. Therefore, Edna must make some choices; but once again they are not entirely free ones, and Edna suffers in consequence. She chooses "the inward life which questions" rather than "the outward existence which conforms" to society's requirements.

Edna Exerts Control Through Her Art

Edna's struggle is symbolized most specifically by her relationship with her husband and with her father. The night after she first heard Mademoiselle Reisz play Chopin, followed by her learning to swim "where no woman had swum before," Edna falls asleep in the hammock. When Léonce asks her to come to bed, she declines, although "another time she would have . . . yielded to his desire . . . unthinking." But now, "she perceived that her will blazed up, stubborn and resistant. She could not at that moment have done other than denied and resisted."

Later, Edna breaks the ritual which she "had religiously followed since her marriage, six years before," by not receiving her Tuesday callers. When Léonce asks her reason, she replies, "I simply felt like going out, and I went out. . . . I left no excuse. I told Joe to say I was out, and that was all." Léonce's only concern—like the later one when she moves out of his houses—is that snubbing wives and daughters will adversely affect his business deals. She can resist, but finally she is powerless. The chapter concludes as Edna flings her wedding ring, the symbol of her bondage, "upon the carpet . . . stamped her heel upon it, striving to crush it. But her small boot heel did not make an indenture." Her lack of power is obvious when, at her maid's bidding, she replaces the ring on her finger. Likewise, Edna's relationship with her father has placed her in a powerless position, although by the time he visits her in New Orleans she has largely escaped his influence. He was "convinced . . . that he had bequeathed to all his daughters the germs of a masterful capability, which only depended upon their own efforts to be directed toward successful achievement"; and, although she had defied him when she married Léonce six years ago, his influence on her personality had been considerable.

However, through art, Edna is able to control her father both literally and symbolically. As she sketches his portrait, "he sat rigid and unflinching, as he had faced the cannon's mouth in days gone by . . . he motioned [the children] away with an expressive action of the foot, loath to disturb the fixed lines of his countenance, his arms, or his rigid shoulders." Literally, then, she makes him rigid, unmovable, confined; and symbolically she shapes him by the act of painting his portrait. In a rather complex symbol, Chopin allows Edna to capture and control her world in painting just as Mlle. Reisz captivates the sensitive with her music. In fact, the courage of the artist is consistently stressed in the image of the bird which soars "above the level plain of tradition and prejudice." Art, then, is an acceptable way—because it appears harmless—for women to express their *selves* in this society, but, as Mlle. Reisz knows well, to succeed as an artist, one "must possess the courageous soul. . . . The soul that dares and defies." Therefore, fortuitously, Edna's artistic temperament and her restless spirit symbolically complement each other. Edna awakens to her true self and defies her society.

Society Was Not Ready for a Free Woman

However, in 1899 the nation was not ready for an "awakened" woman, and Chopin knew this. Although younger and more charming than Edna's husband, Robert her lover is not ready to meet her needs. He admits that he tried not to love her because, he says, "you were not free; you were Léonce Pontellier's wife. . . . I was demented, dreaming of wild, impossible things, recalling men who had set their wives free." Edna's reply:

> "You have been a very, very foolish boy, wasting your time dreaming of impossible things when you speak of Mr. Pontellier setting me free! I am no longer one of Mr. Pontellier's possessions to dispose of or not. I give myself where I choose. If he were to say, 'Here, Robert, take her and be happy; she is yours,' I should laugh at you both."

While Edna attends a birth—another complicated metaphor—Robert leaves a note: "I love you. Good-by—because I love you." Unable either to think of "having" Edna without possessing her, or perhaps to face the censure of society in a divorce or an open love affair, Robert deserts the woman he loves telling himself it is *because* he loves her. Consequently, in an act of obvious defiance, Edna disrobes and walks into the sea while a bird with a broken wing reels and flutters down to the water. Edna's final vision as she drowns is of her father, who in his military uniform is a symbol of authority, discipline, and restraint.

Chopin's literary career ended with Edna's suicide. Readers and critics were not yet ready for her honesty and courage in

Chopin Made a Daring Foray into Female Identity and Sexuality

Joyce Dyer

Joyce Dyer is a professor of English and the director of writing at Hiram College in Ohio. She is a literary critic and an essayist and is the author of a memoir, In a Tangled Wood: An Alzheimer's Journey.

It is only appropriate that Chopin died after attending the St. Louis World's Fair, suggests Joyce Dyer in the following viewpoint. Occurring in 1904, the St. Louis World's Fair combined exhibits celebrating the past and those embracing the future, symbolizing the tension between old and new that existed at the turn of the century. One of these new waves of thought was the first stirrings of feminism, Dyer asserts, as writers and activists began questioning the traditional role of women. Chopin took feminism a step further than her contemporaries, however, in her exploration of female passion in The Awakening, *Dyer claims. Society was not yet ready to accept the erotic nature of women, and reviewers were highly critical of her novel.*

The last event Kate Chopin attended in her life was the St. Louis World's Fair. . . .

The fair, as Chopin may well have sensed, was a perfect symbol of the period during which she wrote. . . . The fair celebrated progress and the present.

But, paradoxically, the fair also celebrated the past, the old, conservative ways and symbols that were quiet and reassuring in restless times. . . .

Joyce Dyer, "Background to the Novel," *The Awakening: A Novel of Beginnings.* Belmont, CA: The Gale Group, 1993, pp. 3–12. Copyright © by The Gale Group. Reproduced by permission.

This tension between the old and the new, between the nineteenth century and the twentieth, the traditional and the modern, always fascinated and challenged Chopin, and she wrote about it in story after story, including *The Awakening*.

The 1890s Saw the Beginning of Feminism

The 1890s were very complicated years; changes occurred in that decade that would permanently alter life as nineteenth-century Americans had known it. The works of [Charles] Darwin, [Herbert] Spencer, and [Thomas] Huxley were transforming intellectual thought. Chopin's friend and contemporary William Schuyler first noted the influence of such thinkers on Chopin. Per Seyersted, who wrote a 1969 biography of Chopin, feels that her reading of science "confirmed her in her belief of the relativity of morals," a theme that certainly surfaces in the behavior of Edna Pontellier. Fixed truth in any form—moral or religious or scientific— seldom escaped Chopin's ironic glance.

In *The Awakening*, of course, it was the fixed idea of women's roles that most concerned Chopin. She and other women were beginning to set down the roots of modern feminism during the 1890s. As the historian Mary Ryan has noted, five million women would join the work force by 1900.

A few strong women were demonstrating new independence in their daily lives. Martha Louise Munger Black left her husband because he would not undertake an adventure to the Klondike in 1898: "I wrote to Will that I had made up my mind to go to the Klondyke [*sic*] as originally planned, that I would never go back to him, so undependable he had proven, that I never wanted to hear from or see him again. He went his way. I went mine." Charmian Kittredge (who married Jack London in 1905) occasionally shocked East Bay society by "her daring rides astride alone in the hills and her familiarity with writers thought to be of questionable morals such as Thomas Hardy and Henrik Ibsen."

Elizabeth Cady Stanton saw her radical work, *The Woman's Bible,* published in 1895—two weeks after her eightieth birthday. Susan B. Anthony, who turned seventy in 1890, campaigned throughout the decade for the enfranchisement of women. . . .

In 1898 Charlotte Perkins Gilman, who was, like Anthony, a member of the National American Woman Suffrage Association, published *Women and Economics,* which advocates women becoming more economically independent, thereby improving their marriages and increasing their own humanity. Gilman felt, as Chopin did, that relationships founded on economic dependence and expectations about the performance of household duties needed to be reexamined. She wrote: "Marriage is not perfect unless it is between class equals. There is no equality in class between those who do their share in the world's work in the largest, newest, highest ways and those who do theirs in the smallest, oldest, lowest ways."

Other writers of the 1890s besides Chopin questioned women's traditional roles. As Larzer Ziff points out in *The American 1890s,* "To be a serious female author in the nineties was to be a writer of stories about women and their demands." Authors like Ellen Glasgow and Theodore Dreiser were looking at the effects of urban living on relationships between men and women, sometimes exploring issues Gilman, too, thought significant. Sarah Orne Jewett was writing about strong friendships between her courageous and honest New England women, not about conventional romances.

Equality Existed in a Narrow Framework

Women in the 1890s, however, including women writers, could be only so bold. Popular culture reflected the nation's suspicion of women who chose untraditional roles. The typewriter, for example, came to represent the evil influence of office work on America's once-domestic women. Thomas Getz in 1889 composed the popular song, "Since My Daughter Plays

An automobile parade at the 1904 St. Louis World's Fair, which Kate Chopin attended shortly before her death. Joyce Dyer argues that the fair's celebration of both past and future was "the perfect symbol of the period during which [Chopin] wrote." Hulton Archive/ Getty Images.

on the Typewriter," in which an Irish father mourns the changes his daughter, Bridget Maguire, has undergone since becoming a typist. . . .

The historians Linda Kerber and Jane S. DeHart explain that even as women were becoming increasingly political in the nineteenth century, increasingly more public, they were doing so almost always under the guise of "Motherhood"—at first, "Republican Motherhood," and later, "Reformist Motherhood" and "Political Motherhood." . . .

The great majority of novels with "subversive" themes nevertheless had acceptable resolutions. Even before the 1890s, a large group of women writers—dubbed the "literary domestics" by the historian Mary Kelley—were focusing on female experience, though largely as defined by the domestic sphere. Ziff, discussing novels of the 1890s, concludes that they often contain fairly strong statements about women's right to equality, but that most offer only timid resolutions. "The new theme of the independent woman called for a new plot that would not resistlessly flow to the magnetic terminal of marriage, but the young lady writers of the nineties dared enough when they dared the theme," he explains. "Their works are marred and sometimes destroyed because they cannot break free of the marriage pattern."

Even the divorced woman—the new woman entering fiction from the mid-nineteenth century on—and the widow often found their salvation in remarriage. . . .

Some single women—or divorced women—in nineteenth-century novels do refuse to marry, or remarry. These women either withdraw from society, like Marcia Hubbard in William Dean Howells's *Modern Instance* (1881), or commit themselves to a righteous cause. . . .

Female Passion Was Still Taboo

Female passion was thought to be immoral and unhealthy by even some of the most aggressive proponents of realism and feminism in the last decades of the nineteenth century. To suggest otherwise was to enter extremely perilous waters, the waters in which Edna herself swims. Consequently, female characters who were separated from men—by their unmarried status, their disillusionment with husbands, or divorce— seldom considered the avenue of liberated sexual behavior an option.

The 1890s was the decade, we must remember, when audiences were scandalized by the first long embrace on the screen in *The John Rice-May Irwin Kiss.* R.W. Gilder, the editor of *Century*—one of the most important literary magazines of the decade, it published [Mark] Twain, [William Dean] Howells, Chopin, [Jack] London, and [Edith] Wharton—frequently encouraged his authors to make their stories more pleasing (that is, more morally wholesome and sweet). Although Howells created the famous image of a real rather than ideal grasshopper to register his preference for what is true, he was careful to provide his own definition of realistic truth. Howells admired American novelists who avoided writing books like [Leo Tolstoy's] *Anna Karenina* (1873) and [Gustave Flaubert's] *Madame Bovary* (1857). Such books, Howells thought, were "cheap and meretricious" and lacked fidelity to "feeling and character" because they focus so heavily on just one passion rather than on the many that exist—on just "the passion of guilty love."

Even Charlotte Perkins Gilman, one of the most radical voices of the decade, spoke out strongly against female eroticism. We might guess that the far more enthusiastic reception of Gilman's text over Chopin's was related to Gilman's conservative position on sexual issues. For Gilman, sex was useful for reproduction only; what she called "excessive sex-indulgence" (caused in her opinion by abnormal "sex-distinction") functioned only "to pervert and exhaust desire as well as to injure reproduction." Gilman defended the sanctity of marriage (however radically modified a form of it), along with the sanctity of monogamy and fidelity. Life's greatest evil, Gilman claimed, consisted of "promiscuous and temporary sex-relations."

In a decade that made Charles M. Sheldon's *In His Steps: "What Would Jesus Do?"* (1896) one of its most popular books, it was not surprising to hear frequent warnings about sex also coming from the country's pulpits. Thomas DeWitt Talmage, one of the most influential and severe pulpit speakers of his day, shouted out the dangers of immoral literature—of books that made "impurity decent." And what should good Christians do who find themselves in possession of such unprincipled volumes? "Kindle a fire on your kitchen hearth," he advised, "or in your back yard, and then drop the poison in it, and keep stirring the blaze until from preface to appendix there shall not be a single paragraph left, and the bonfire in your city shall be as consuming as that one in the streets of Ephesus." [A bonfire destroyed the Temple of Artemis in the Greek city of Ephesus, which Christians interpreted as punishment for idolatry.] Thus were the early beginnings of feminism in America linked with eternal damnation. . . .

New Orleans Was a Conservative City

To have a full sense of the shock Edna's behavior causes other characters in the novel—and caused Chopin's own reviewers—we need to remember that New Orleans, where much of *The Awakening* is set, had a triple history: it was, of course, American in many senses, but it was also southern and Creole. New Orleans felt the energy and changes of the nation. Margaret Culley notes that the 1890s brought hints of the women's movement to the Crescent City. Susan B. Anthony, for example, visited New Orleans in 1895. Women were entering new professions, becoming barbers, undertakers, cigar importers, insurance agents, and liquor dealers.

Nevertheless, Louisiana remained an extremely conservative state. In 1808 Louisiana adopted the *Digest of the Civil Laws Now in Force in the Territory of Orleans*, patterned on the *Code Napoleon* of France. The Louisiana Code, which firmly established the husband as the head of the family, was still determining the conditions of marriage contracts at the end of the century. According to article 1388 of the code, the patriarchal structure of the Louisiana family was not a negotiable matter. And in article 1124 married women, along with babies and the mentally deranged, were declared incompetent to make contracts.

Marie Fletcher, describing the depiction of Louisiana women in local color fiction, writes, "Basically they have much in common with the genteel ladies of the past, for they still represent the ideal of the fragile and lovely girl who is pure of character." In their report to the Louisiana Purchase Exposition Commission in 1905, the Board of Lady Managers, chaired by Mary Margaretta Manning, continued to take its greatest pride in the creation of a social center on the exposition grounds, "their province being that of *National* Hostesses,—their privilege to extend a generous and far-reaching hospitality to all official dignitaries from home and abroad who visited the Exposition." They were not, like Edna, questioning the importance of such afternoon receptions.

The Creole women of Louisiana, though seemingly less constrained than other women, were actually among the most conservative members of their sex in the nineteenth century. Like Adèle, they were frank and physical. But it was their unquestionable personal and religious commitment to family, chastity, husband, and children that made this open manner possible. For them, Mary Shaffter wrote in 1892, "women's rights . . . are the right to love and be loved, and to name the babies rather than the next president or city officials." Edna, not a Catholic but a Presbyterian, not a Creole but a southerner, adopts the candor and sensual manner of her Creole friends yet leaves their traditional notions of wifehood and motherhood behind.

Society Was Not Ready for Bold Sexuality

The tensions between the old and the new, the traditional and the untraditional, were great during the final years of the nineteenth century. It is not surprising that a country faced with such difficult and complex questions would sometimes turn to sentiment and easy answers for escape. Americans of the 1890s adored Reginald DeKoven's light opera *Robin Hood* (1890) (which ran for 3,000 performances), Joel Chandler

Harris's *Nights with Uncle Remus* (1892), Margaret M. Saunders's classic dog tale, *Beautiful Joe* (1894), and John Philip Sousa's "The Stars and Stripes Forever" (1896). The year 1900 would see the publication of L. Frank Baum's *The Wonderful Wizard of Oz* (adapted for the stage in 1901) and Beatrix Potter's *The Tale of Peter Rabbit.*

The St. Louis World's Fair, with its displays and exhibits of both the old and the new, was the perfect event to bridge two centuries. Chopin lived during that transitional time. Her work offers the promise of new beginnings, but never the false promise that it will be easy. It is sadly appropriate that Chopin died after a day at the fair—literally and metaphorically, her fascination with the tension the fair displayed had a hand in killing her. Both as a visitor to the fair and as a writer she risked security and safety in the pursuit of change and exploration. Boldness drove Chopin to the fairgrounds on a day when the sun was too severe. Boldness also led her to compose *The Awakening* at the wrong time: when reviewers were ready for neither the questions she asked nor the study of females in transition that she eloquently and painfully undertook.

Chopin's Artistry Is Wasted on Her Sordid Subject

Willa Cather

Willa Cather was a Pulitzer Prize–winning author of novels set in the Great Plains. Among her most celebrated works are My Ántonia *and* Oh Pioneers!

The heroines of The Awakening *and Gustave Flaubert's* Madame Bovary *belong to the same unfortunate class of woman— those who are ruled by their passions—Willa Cather writes in this early review of* The Awakening. *Kate Chopin is a gifted author, with the ability to write simply and with great sensitivity, Cather states. It is lamentable that she chose such an unworthy subject for her superb prose.*

A Creole Bovary is this little novel of Miss Chopin's. Not that the heroine is a creole exactly, or that Miss Chopin is a [Gustave] Flaubert—save the mark!—but the theme is similar to that which occupied Flaubert. There was, indeed, no need that a second *Madame Bovary* [by Flaubert] should be written, but an author's choice of themes is frequently as inexplicable as his choice of a wife. It is governed by some innate temperamental bias that cannot be diagrammed. This is particularly so in women who write, and I shall not attempt to say why Miss Chopin has devoted so exquisite and sensitive, well-governed a style to so trite and sordid a theme. She writes much better than it is ever given to most people to write, and hers is a genuinely literary style; of no great elegance or solidity; but light, flexible, subtle and capable of producing telling effects directly and simply. The story she has to tell in the present instance is new neither in matter nor treatment. "Edna

Pontellier," a Kentucky girl, who, like "Emma Bovary," had been in love with innumerable dream heroes before she was out of short skirts, married "Leonce Pontellier" as a sort of reaction from a vague and visionary passion for a tragedian whose unresponsive picture she used to kiss. She acquired the habit of liking her husband in time, and even of liking her children. Though we are not justified in presuming that she ever threw articles from her dressing table at them, as the charming "Emma" had a winsome habit of doing, we are told that "she would sometimes gather them passionately to her heart, she would sometimes forget them." At a Creole watering place, which is admirably and deftly sketched by Miss Chopin, "Edna" met "Robert Lebrun," son of the landlady, who dreamed of a fortune awaiting him in Mexico while he occupied a petty clerical position in New Orleans. "Robert" made it his business to be agreeable to his mother's boarders, and "Edna," not being a Creole, much against his wish and will, took him seriously. "Robert" went to Mexico but found that fortunes were no easier to make there than in New Orleans. He returns and does not even call to pay his respects to her. She encounters him at the home of a friend and takes him home with her. She wheedles him into staying for dinner, and we are told she sent the maid off "in search of some delicacy she had not thought of for herself, and she recommended great care in the dripping of the coffee and having the omelet done to a turn."

Edna Pontellier Is a Literary Type

Only a few pages back we were informed that the husband, "M. Pontellier," had cold soup and burnt fish for his dinner. Such is life. The lover of course disappointed her, was a coward and ran away from his responsibilities before they began. He was afraid to begin a chapter with so serious and limited a woman. She remembered the sea where she had first met "Robert." Perhaps from the same motive which threw "Anna

Portrait of American author Willa Cather (1873–1947), taken near the turn of the twentieth century. In her 1899 review of The Awakening, *Cather praises Chopin's writing style but finds the book's subject matter "trite and sordid."* Fotoresearch/Getty Images.

Karenina" [in the novel by the same name by Leo Tolstoy] under the engine wheels, she threw herself into the sea, swam until she was tired and then let go.

She looked into the distance, and for a moment the old terror flamed up, then sank again. She heard her father's voice, and her sister Margaret's. She heard the barking of an old dog that was chained to the sycamore tree. The spurs of the cavalry officer clanged as he walked across the porch. There was a hum of bees, and the musky odor of pinks filled the air.

"Edna Pontellier" and "Emma Bovary" are studies in the same feminine type; one a finished and complete portrayal, the other a hasty sketch, but the theme is essentially the same. Both women belong to a class, not large, but forever clamoring in our ears, that demands more romance out of life than God put into it. [British playwright] Mr. G. Bernard Shaw would say that they are the victims of the over-idealization of love. They are the spoil of the poets, the [Greek tragic heroine] Iphigenias of sentiment. The unfortunate feature of their disease is that it attacks only women of brains, at least of rudimentary brains, but whose development is one-sided; women of strong and fine intuitions, but without the faculty of observation, comparison, reasoning about things. Probably, for emotional people, the most convenient thing about being able to think is that it occasionally gives them a rest from feeling. Now with women of the "Bovary" type, this relaxation and recreation is impossible. They are not critics of life, but, in the most personal sense, partakers of life. They receive impressions through the fancy [imagination]. With them everything begins with fancy, and passions rise in the brain rather than in the blood, the poor, neglected, limited one-sided brain that might do so much better things than badgering itself into frantic endeavors to love. For these are the people who pay with their blood for the fine ideals of the poets, as Marie Delclasse paid in [Alexandre] Dumas' great creation, "Marguerite Gauthier." These people really expect the passion of love to fill and gratify every need of life, whereas nature only intended that it should meet one of many demands. They insist upon making it stand for all the emotional pleasures of life and art, expecting an individual and self-limited passion to yield infinite variety, pleasure and distraction, to contribute to their lives what the arts and the pleasurable exercise of the intellect gives to less limited and less intense idealists. So this passion, when set up against [William] Shakespeare, [Honoré de] Balzac, [Richard] Wagner, Raphael [a Renaissance artist], fails them. They have staked everything on one hand, and they lose. They have driven the blood until it will drive no further, they have played their nerves up to the point where any relaxation short of absolute annihilation is impossible. Every idealist abuses his nerves, and every sentimentalist brutally abuses them. And in the end, the nerves get even. Nobody ever cheats them, really. Then "the awakening" comes. Sometimes it comes in the form of arsenic, as it came to "Emma Bovary," sometimes it is carbolic acid taken covertly in the police station, a goal to which unbalanced idealism not infrequently leads. "Edna Pontellier," fanciful and romantic to the last, chose the sea on a summer night and went down with the sound of her first lover's spurs in her ears, and the scent of pinks about her. And next time I hope that Miss Chopin will devote that flexible, iridescent style of hers to a better cause.

Women's Inequality Is Shown by Attitudes About Sexuality in *The Awakening*

Anna Shannon Elfenbein

Anna Shannon Elfenbein teaches women's studies, American literature, and film at West Virginia University.

Edna yearns for an authentic existence in The Awakening, *but she is ultimately trapped by her own lack of empathy, Anna Shannon Elfenbein argues in the following viewpoint. She is able to defy the conventions of her era and fulfill her sexual nature. However, she is also a victim of society's conventions. Coming from a sheltered existence, Edna makes the fatal mistakes of misreading her lover's intentions, cutting herself off from her female friends, and totally ignoring the black women around her, the author contends.*

At the turn of the century, Edna stands alone, for while male authors such as Stephen Crane, Hamlin Garland, and Theodore Dreiser broached the subject of women's sexuality, they permitted sexual passion only to lower-class women and generally maintained a point of view detached from their characters' sexual experience. Edna is unique because her creator was female and because Edna is a white, upper-class wife and mother. Crane's Maggie (*Maggie: A Girl of the Streets* [1893]), Garland's Rose (*Rose of Dutcher's Coolly* [1895]), and Dreiser's Carrie (*Sister Carrie* [1900]) manifest passion, but only Edna gains an independent sense of herself as a sexual being; and she defies race, class, and gender conventions re-

Anna Shannon Elfenbein, "Kate Chopin: From Stereotype to Sexual Realism," in *Women on the Color Line: Evolving Stereotypes and the Writings of George Washington Cabel, Grace King, Kate Chopin.* Charlottesville, VA: University of Virginia Press, 1989, pp. 142–44, 150–52, 157. Copyright © 1989 by University of Virginia Press. Reproduced by permission.

garding woman's sexual nature as she moves by fits and starts to a partial understanding of the obstacles to her personal freedom and fulfillment.

Potential for Empathy Destroyed

The chief obstacle to freedom of expression for Edna, as Chopin dramatizes her plight, is the social status and class perspective that destroy Edna's potential for empathy. It is therefore not until the penultimate episode and Edna's rending recollection of her own participation in childbirth that she can generalize her experience of the delusive and disabling effects of white female privilege. Edna's lack of empathy is so profound that some readers of the novel recoil from her. However, Chopin shows this lack to be in part the product of a domestic routine that deadens Edna's ability to feel, except as she and other privileged white women have been programmed to feel. Such a routine eliminates the possibility of subversive thoughts or vital connections with the experience of other women. Bound by her sex, class, and race to a narrow existence, Edna is defined by those assumptions about women she seeks vainly to escape. Presuming to speak for all women but clearly wishing to be regarded as the exception, Edna remarks, "We women learn so little of life on the whole." This negative view of those with whom she shares a stigmatized status retards the intellectual and emotional development she requires to survive.

The novel repeatedly stresses Edna's inability to know herself or those around her. From first to last she relies on "obstructed" vision, and despite her "natural aptitude" as an artist, she never draws a convincing likeness; nor does her perceptual field encompass the richly textured and gregarious Creole society she inhabits. In contrast to George Cable's Frowenfeld, Edna, a Protestant Kentuckian, fails to understand the racial realities of Creole society or to recognize the dangers posed by Creole difference. Instead she is the "solitary soul" of Chopin's original title. As Margaret Culley notes, "the word *alone* resounds like a refrain in the text, occurring some two dozen times." The key scenes in the novel are Edna's epiphanies. Edna's contemplation of her existence begins and ends, says Culley, in the "'abyss of solitude' which is the sea." Striving for individual transcendence, Edna discovers the bounds of her prison, coterminous with those confining other women. But because her thinking, including a negative view of her own sex, is grounded in convention, her solitary insights are unfocused, dissolving until her final awakening in a mist of genuine feeling, suffused with romantic illusions about a completely conventional lover.

Edna's illusions about love merge with her misperceptions of the women surrounding her, leaving her to face her final awakening alone. She fails to know her friends, Madame Ratignolle, a Creole "mother-woman" who lives only for and through her growing family, and Mademoiselle Reisz, a "liberated" woman who sacrifices every social and personal amenity for her art, but who can only perform music written by male composers. She also fails to note the dark women who predominate in her society. Although her "white solipsism" resembles that of others of her class, her failure to see the women on the margins of her social world ultimately proves fatal, since they direct attention to the illusions animating her belief in transcendent passion. Because they disclose the division of oppression that determines women's life chances in the novel, Edna's blindness to them must be seen as disabling. Thus, although she defies the prescriptions that define the white woman's purity and the dark woman's passion, she finally fails to achieve more than the partial, objectifying vision of woman's nature afforded by convention. . . .

Edna's Limited Existence

Three scenes from the novel illustrate the unequal power of husband and wife in patriarchal marriage and depict Edna's faltering attempts to take possession of the self she begins to discover at Chênière Caminada. They culminate in Edna's confrontation with one of the dark women in her household, who reminds her of her place as wife. Edna's confrontation with this woman, the most direct of a series of confrontations with dark women who shadow her throughout the novel, anticipates later confrontations that confirm Edna's place as a mother and as a sexual being in a society where only men and dark women are sexual beings. In this society Edna's chief function is to evidence wasted effort in caring for her children, seeing to the meals, acting as a willing but undemanding sexual partner for her husband, and discharging her husband's social obligations in a creditable manner. The parameters of her privilege are as rigidly defined as those of the menials and rivals she fails to see.

In the first scene, Léonce takes Edna to task for her "habitual neglect" of the children. He has returned late from a gambling evening at Klein's hotel and demands her attention, although she is sleeping. The real issue, however, is revealed by Léonce's chagrin that Edna, "the sole object of his existence, evinced so little interest in things which concerned him, and valued so little his conversation." When she continues to be unresponsive, Léonce informs her that Raoul has a high fever. Since it is "a mother's place to look after children," Léonce leaves Edna to attend Raoul and finishes his bedtime cigar in peace. Thoroughly awake, Edna springs out of bed to see to Raoul, who, she knows, is quite well. Edna's acceptance of Léonce's devaluation of her as a mother appears in her inability to express her anger at Léonce's behavior and in the fact that "she could not have told why she was crying. Such experiences as the foregoing were not uncommon in her married life. They seemed never before to have weighed much against the abundance of her husband's kindness and a uniform devotion which had come to be tacit and self-understood."

In the second scene, Edna resists Léonce's sexual importunities. Having settled into a hammock outside to contemplate the significance of her first swim, Edna refuses Léonce's request, his entreaty, and finally his command to come to bed. Still unable to formulate a rationale for resistance, Edna nevertheless recognizes that she has made a significant break with her past, a break that will make subsequent breaks inevitable. Just as she once walked the "daily treadmill of the life" that had been portioned out to her as Léonce's wife, in resistance Edna becomes once more the object of forces she little understands. At the moment of her most intense self-assertion, she is at the mercy of uncontrollable emotion: "She could not at that moment have done other than denied and resisted. She wondered if her husband had ever spoken to her like that before, and if she had submitted to his command. Of course she had; she remembered that she had. But she could not realize why or how she should have yielded, feeling as she then did."

The Man Is the Victor

The intensity of Edna's emotion and her conviction fade when Léonce intrudes on her vigil with a glass of wine and a cigar. "Like one who awakens gradually out of a dream, a delicious, grotesque, impossible dream, to feel again the realities pressing into her soul," Edna finally asks, "Are you coming in, Léonce?" Léonce's smug reply testifies to his sense of his victory: "Yes, dear. . . . Just as soon as I have finished my cigar."

In the third scene, following the return to New Orleans from the summer freedom of Grand Isle, Léonce wins again. Edna's resistance emerges to the social rituals she has "religiously followed since her marriage, six years before," when she fails to be at home on her Tuesday reception day to receive the wives of Léonce's business acquaintances. At dinner Léonce defends "*les convenances*" against such assaults and vents his anger at Edna for failing to manage the cook so that he could "procure at least one meal a day which a man could eat and retain his self-respect." Edna, however, lacks contrition, although "on a few previous occasions she had been completely deprived of any desire to finish her dinner. Sometimes she had gone into the kitchen to administer a tardy rebuke to the cook. Once she went to her room and studied the cookbook during an entire evening, finally writing out a menu for the week, which left her harassed with a feeling that, after all, she had accomplished no good that was worth the name."

Notwithstanding her growing consciousness of the triviality of her functions as Léonce's wife, Edna's resistance is futile, for when she takes off her wedding ring and flings it to the carpet, her small boot heel cannot make even "an indenture, not a mark upon the little glittering circlet." When, in frustration, she throws a vase on the hearth, a maid enters to remind her of her position as Mrs. Pontellier. Submitting to this dark woman as she submitted to Léonce earlier, Edna holds "out her hand, and taking the ring, slipped it upon her finger."

Caring for Edna as she cares for the other possessions in Léonce Pontellier's household, the maid extends the reach of Léonce's power by reenacting his gesture with Edna's wedding ring. Edna's response to the maid signals once more her blind resignation to the relationships that perpetuate her husband's power over her. For if she cannot govern herself or her servants, she lacks the capacity both for her role and for the rebellion she contemplates.

Unrecognized Consequences

With this final scene, the revolt that began at Grand Isle has touched the whole of Edna's social world, from her disappointed callers to the servants in her home. But the revolt has achieved nothing of substance, as her resignation at the end of this scene discloses. Edna's flickering insight into her situation compounds her problem. Her ability to conclude "that it was very foolish, very childish, to have stamped upon her wedding ring and smashed the crystal vase upon the tiles" is compromised by the "spell of her infatuation" with Robert Lebrun, which colors her perception of the possibilities of fulfillment and leads her to await "life's delirium." Similarly, the sharpness of her reported assertion that "a wedding is one of the most lamentable spectacles on earth" loses conviction because she lends herself to "any passing caprice" in an attempt to avoid coming to terms with her situation.

Although her aimless responses do not invalidate her experience, Edna repeatedly avoids confronting the implications of her actions. Thus, she emerges at the feast to celebrate her independence crowned by Léonce's gift of "a magnificent cluster of diamonds that sparkled, that almost sputtered." Later, although beyond the point of reconciliation, she answers Léonce's letter concerning a projected family trip to Europe with "friendly evasiveness,—not with any fixed design to mislead him, only because all sense of reality had gone out of her life."

Edna's inability to continue complying with her social role as a Victorian wife merges with her inability to focus on the implications for her of a fully realized sexuality. Adèle's chronic "condition," Mademoiselle Reisz's spinsterhood, and Léonce's repeated trips to his club, however, signal what was the Victorian woman's primary existential choice: pregnancy, celibacy, or continence in marriage, maintained at her expense by the double standard.

Edna's inability to respond in the accepted Victorian way to motherhood, "that outward and visible sign of the angelic condition of wifehood," foreshadows her ultimate awakening to the biological trap sprung by sexual desire. Initially, Edna's vague distrust of the way in which Adèle exploits her "condition" fails to penetrate the falseness of the sentimental image; Edna never notices the presence of quadroon women who maintain the illusion that Adèle serves. . . .

Divisive Romantic Illusions

In the ambivalent final chapter of *The Awakening*, as in the beginning, Edna is Mrs. Pontellier. Intruding upon Mariequita and Victor, to whom she gives orders for a supper she never intends to eat, she betrays once again her programming as a privileged white woman. Through food, the emblem of her subjugation and her self-indulgence throughout the novel, Edna establishes her claim on Mariequita, the dark woman she needs to provide a plausible story of her accidental drowning. Mariequita will provide that story, for she believes in the mythic Edna, Victor's construct—a woman "who gave the most sumptuous dinners in America, and who had all the men in New Orleans at her feet." Mariequita's belief in the mythic Edna reconfirms the potency and prevalence of the romantic illusions that divide women from each other. A final contrast to Edna, who detaches herself from story-making and story-hearing by committing suicide, Mariequita survives untouched by Edna's awakening. In the world of the novel, the conventions Chopin challenged remain to motivate mythmaking and to preclude for all women a full awakening to life's possibilities.

The Awakening Shows the Destructive Nature of Victorian Notions of Women's Sexuality

Cynthia Griffin Wolff

Cynthia Griffin Wolff is a professor of humanities at Massachusetts Institute of Technology and the author or editor of a number of books of literary criticism and biography, including Emily Dickinson.

The medical profession of the nineteenth century promulgated the mistaken belief that it was abnormal for women to have sexual feelings and that the only reason that a decent woman embraced her sexuality was to bear children, explains Cynthia Griffin Wolff in the following viewpoint. Chopin challenged these assumptions in The Awakening, *argues Wolff, affirming the right of women to independent existence as sexual beings. Ahead of its time,* The Awakening *was first criticized and then ignored, but Chopin has finally been vindicated as her novel is now recognized as a masterpiece, maintains Wolff.*

After about 1849, the notion of a "woman's sexual awakening" became, by definition, an impossibility—a contradiction in terms—because the medical establishment in America began to promulgate the view that normal females possessed no erotic inclinations whatsoever (and one cannot awaken something that does not exist). William Acton, the acknowledged expert on the nature of women's sexuality and author of "one of the most widely quoted books on sexual problems and diseases in the English-speaking world," wrote:

Cynthia Griffin Wolff, "Un-Utterable Longing: The Discourse of Feminine Sexuality in *The Awakening," Studies in American Fiction*, 24.1, 1996, pp. 3–23. Copyright © 1996 by Studies in American Fiction. Reproduced by permission.

I have taken pains to obtain and compare abundant evidence on this subject, and the result of my inquiries I may briefly epitomize as follows:—I should say that the majority of women (happily for society) are not very much troubled with sexual feeling of any kind. What men are habitually women are only exceptionally. It is too true, I admit, as the divorce courts show, that there are some few women who have sexual desires so strong that they surpass those of men, and shock public feeling by their consequences.

Acton's work elaborated a comprehensive system of women's "inequality" to men; and it was so universally respected that his sentiments can be taken to represent opinions that were held throughout much of America during the second half of the nineteenth century. Certainly they define the attitudes of that stern Presbyterian world in which Edna Pontellier grew to maturity.

In fact, Edna's particular religious background could not have been chosen casually by Chopin, for a woman reared in this faith during the 1870s and 1880s (the years of Edna's youth) would have been preternaturally susceptible to the most crippling elements of Acton's strictures. . . .

Normal Women Are Not Sexual

All of Acton's formulations are sweepingly comprehensive and inescapably normative, and in this respect he greatly resembles the Puritans. He does not admit of gradations among women; nor does he entertain the possibility that additional data—testimony from women themselves, perhaps—might contradict or even emend his pronouncements. Instead, he presents his ideas as nothing less than a description of both a divinely ordained condition and a condition for middle-class respectability. He clearly considers the absence of passion in "normal women" to be a good thing (for its presence in a decent female would "shock public feeling"); and he refers dismissively to "prostitutes" and "loose, or, at least, low and vulgar women"

The cover of a paperback edition of Kate Chopin's The Awakening. *HarperCollins Publishers.*

whose strong libidinous drives "give a very false idea of the condition of female sexual feelings in general." In short, the innate frigidity of women signified a form of refinement and could be used as a touchstone for respectability.

The official "scientific" and "medical" view can be stated quite simply: an average woman (a "decent" woman) possesses no sexual feelings whatsoever. Thus it is not enough to say that *The Awakening* is a novel about repression (that is, about a situation in which a woman possesses sexual feelings, but is prohibited from acting upon them). It is, instead, a novel about a woman whose shaping culture has, in general, refused her right to speak out freely; this is, moreover, a culture that construes a woman's self-expression as a violation of sexual "purity" and a culture that has denied the existence of women's libidinous potential altogether—has eliminated the very concept of sexual passion for "normal" women.

The consequences are emotionally mutilating (in the extreme case, some form of mental breakdown would result). In such a culture, if a "respectable" woman supposes herself to feel "something," some powerful ardor in her relationship with a man, she can draw only two possible inferences. Either her feelings are not sexual (and should not be enacted in a genital relationship), or she is in some (disgraceful) way "abnormal." Moreover, because there is presumed to be no such entity as sexual feelings in the typical woman, a typical (i.e. "normal") woman will literally have no words for her (nonexistent) feelings, will have access to no discourse within which these (nonexistent) passions can be examined or discussed, will be able to make no coherent connection between the (unintelligible) inner world of her affective life and the external, social world in which she must live. Finally, if she feels confusion and emotional pain, her culture's general prohibition against speaking out will make it difficult, perhaps impossible, to discuss or even reveal her discomfort.

Of course there was an escape hatch (infinitesimal and insufficient). After all, men and women did marry, did have sexual intercourse, doubtless did (sometimes) enjoy their lovemaking, and did (occasionally) find ways to discuss the intimate elements of their relationship. Indeed, the range of actual situations for females in America at the end of the nineteenth century—among various cultural groups, among diverse regions—was undoubtedly rather great. Yet the normative pronouncements regarding women's "proper" behavior in this age of Anthony Comstock (founder of the Society for the Suppression of Vice and the man who succeeded in having the Act which bears his name passed in 1873) were stringent—as were the assumptions about public behavior.

Women Do Desire Having Children

The extent and resourcefulness of individual solutions to this situation must remain a mystery. However, the publicly approved forms of discourse for female desire are a matter of record. Medical and psychological experts concluded that although women had no sexual drives per se, they often possessed a passionate desire to bear children: such ardor was both "normal" and (inevitably) sexual. On these terms, then, sexual activity—even moderate sexual "desire"—was appropriate in "normal" women. However, a profound displacement or confusion was introduced by this accommodation: the language of feminine sexuality became inextricably intertwined with discourse that had to do with child-bearing and motherhood.

According to Acton (and others who followed his lead), nature itself had made the longing to have children the essential, causative force of a woman's sexual "appetite." Thus men and women were essentially different: men have sexual impulses and needs (and these are quite independent of any wish to sire offspring); women crave children (and consequently they might be said—very indirectly—to "want" sexual activity). "Virility" and "maternity" were defined as parallel instincts that were nonetheless fundamentally dissimilar; and a woman's possessing sexual ardor independent of her yearning for babies became a defining symptom of abnormality or immorality or both. . . .

Scholars have accepted almost as cliché the fact that in late Victorian America "motherhood" was exalted as an all-but-divine state. However, if we do not also understand the oblique (and contradictory) sexual implications of this cultural ideal, we may be unaware of the confusion and conflict it engendered.

This definition of feminine sexuality radically displaced a woman's passionate desires: unlike males, who were permitted to "possess" their sexuality and were consequently allowed to experience passion directly and as a part of the "self," females were allowed access to sexuality only indirectly—as a subsidiary component of the desire for children. It was literally unimaginable that any "decent" woman would experience sexual appetite as an immediate and urgent drive, distinct from all other desires and duties. In emotional terms, men "owned" their libido; however, women's libido was "owned" by their prospective children.

Confusing Eroticism of Creole Society

Any woman would find this concatenation of denials and demands unbalancing; however, in Edna's case, the already vexed situation is heightened by a severe conflict of cultures. In a society where the actual experiences of women were diverse and the normative pronouncements were stringent, Chopin has constructed a novel where extremes converge to demonstrate the malignant potential of these normative attitudes, and she marks the summer at Grand Isle as the moment when crisis begins.

Reared as a Presbyterian in Kentucky, Edna has been married to a Creole for many years. Nonetheless, she has never-become "thoroughly at home in the society of Creoles; [and] never before had she been thrown so intimately among them." It is not that these people do not have a rigorous sexual code: their customs follow the boundary conditions that Acton and his fellow theorists postulated. However, far from being Bible-bound, sober, and staid, so long as they remain within the rules of this code, Creoles permit themselves an extraordinary freedom of sensual expression. Thus a lusty carnal appetite in men is taken for granted. (Robert has his affair with the Mexican girl, everyone knows about it, and no one thinks to disapprove.) However, the case of Creole women is different, for their sexuality may exist only as a component of "motherhood." Nevertheless, so long as they accept this model, women, too, may engage in a sumptuous sexual life. Mme. Ratignolle, the "sensuous Madonna," embodies the essence of ardor and voluptuary appetite thus construed.

Such a system imposes penalties (Adele's accouchement [being confined to bed] is one specific marker for the price to be paid); however, within these limiting conditions, the Creole world is more densely erotic than any community Edna has encountered. It revels frankly and happily in the pleasures of the flesh—not merely enjoying these delights with undisguised zest, but discussing them in public with no shame at all. Edna can recognize the inherent "chastity" of such people, but their habits nonetheless embarrass her profoundly:

> Madame Ratignolle had been married seven years. About every two years she had a baby. At that time she had three babies, and was beginning to think of a fourth one. She was always talking about her "condition." Her "condition" was in no way apparent, and no one would have known a thing about it but for her persistence in making it the subject of conversation.

A late twentieth century reader may innocently suppose that Adele's preoccupation is purely maternal. The full truth is quite otherwise: in the discourse of the day, Adele has elected to flaunt her sexuality—to celebrate both her ardor and her physical enjoyment. Robert enters the festive, flirtatious moment by recalling the "lady who had subsisted upon nougat during the entire—," and is checked only by Edna's blushing discomfort.

Edna Rejects the Roles Open to Her

All such instances of candor unsettle Mrs. Pontellier. This strange world, with its languorous climate and frankly sensuous habits, is a world where "normal," "respectable" women openly vaunt pleasures that are unfamiliar to Edna Pontellier. She is fascinated, stimulated, eventually profoundly aroused. And although she is bewildered by these new sensations, once having been touched by them, she becomes unwilling to pull away. Much of the novel . . . is concerned with Edna's quest for a viable and acceptable mode of owning and expressing her sexuality: first by locating the defining boundaries for these feelings and thus being able to define and name what she feels inside herself; second by finding some acceptable social construct which will permit her to enact what she feels in the outside world and to make an appropriate, vital, and affirming connection between the "me" and the "not-me."

Edna's easiest option is "collusion," to become a "mother-woman"; however, she rejects this role violently because of the displacements and forfeitures that it would impose. If, like Adele, she were willing to disguise her erotic drives in the mantle of "motherhood," she might indulge the many delights of the body as Adele patently does. However, such a capitulation would not allow her really to possess her own feelings—nor even to talk about them directly or explicitly. It would maim the "self," not unify and affirm it: like Adele, Edna would be obliged to displace all of her sexual discourse into prattle about "the children" or her (pregnant) "condition," fettering her carnal desires to the production of babies; and part of what was really inside (that is, her sexual drive) would have been displaced on to something outside (society's construction of female appetite as essentially "maternal"). In the process, the authority and integrity of her identity would have been compromised, and instead of making contact with the outside world, she would be merged into and controlled by it. Edna loves her children and is happy to be a mother; however, she refuses to define her sexuality in terms of them.

Thus Edna's rejection of this emotional mutilation lies behind the novel's many tortured examinations of her relationship to the children and informs such assertions as: "I would give up the unessential; I would give my money, I would give my life for my children; but I wouldn't give myself." Edna's children make very few actual demands upon her time or energy (and she has all the "childcare" one might desire). Thus the emphatic quality of her renunciation addresses not a real burden, but the internalized social directive. Renouncing what she can clearly recognize as an unacceptable violation of her emotional integrity is Edna's most confident step toward freedom.

She shrugs away from marriage for many of the same reasons, declaring that she will "never again belong to another than herself." The problem is neither immediate nor personal: it is not Leonce, per se, that Edna repudiates, but the warped forms of intimacy that he represents. . . .

Women Are Denied a Voice by Society

[The] dispassionate tone of Chopin's novel may be related to the complexity of Edna's quest, for Edna cannot "solve" her problem without an extraordinary feat of creativity. She must discover not merely a new vernacular with which to name her feelings—not merely a new form of plot that is capable of containing them—but also an "audience" that both comprehends and esteems the story she might ultimately tell. Thus the true subject of *The Awakening* may be less the particular dilemma of Mrs. Pontellier than the larger problems of female narrative that it reflects; and if Edna's poignant fate is in part a reflection of her own habits, it is also, in equal part, a measure of society's failure to allow its women a language of their own. . . .

So Edna has failed. Or rather, being a woman with some weaknesses and no extraordinary strengths, Edna has chosen the only alternative she could imagine to the ravaging social arrangements of her day. (Only seven years earlier, [a short story by Charlotte Perkins Gilman called] "The Yellow Wallpaper" had attracted wide attention to the same stifling, potentially annihilating constructions of "femininity.") However, we must not overlook the fact that if her heroine faltered, Kate Chopin fashioned a splendid success. *The Awakening* is the new narrative that Mrs. Pontellier was unable to create: not (it is true) a story of female affirmation, but rather an excruciatingly exact dissection of the ways in which society distorts a woman's true nature. The ruthless contemporary reviews leave no doubt that Kate Chopin had invented a powerful (and thus threatening) discourse for feminine sexuality. And although the novel was forced to languish (Like yet another "sleeping beauty") largely unread for three quarters of a century, the current respect it enjoys is a belated affirmation of Kate Chopin's *success.*

Edna Recognizes the Importance of Freedom but Is Unable to Attain It

Barbara C. Ewell

Barbara C. Ewell is the Dorothy Harrell Brown Distinguished Professor of English at Loyola University. She is the coeditor of several collections on the literature of the American South, including Voices of the American South.

The Awakening *is a complex book that, raising serious questions about the nature of female sexuality and the boundaries of free will and inherited destiny, concludes that there are no easy answers, maintains Barbara C. Ewell in the following viewpoint. Addressing the fundamental issue of how a woman achieves selfhood in a restrictive society, Chopin portrays a flawed Edna realizing the need for an authentic existence, but failing to attain it, in Ewell's view.*

[T]he] central issue of Chopin's last novel [*The Awakening*] is one she had addressed in her first: how does one (especially one female) achieve personal integrity in a world of conventional restraints? It is a problem Chopin constantly confronted as a writer; and the solutions at which she arrived implied both compromise and failure, embodying her vision in conventional motifs and styles, articulating it through familiar and acceptable materials. But while no writer manages to express her vision purely, without some accommodation of literary conventions and commercial expectations, by this point Chopin had developed, in the expressive fidelity of her style, a subtle vehicle for the complex realities she perceived.

Barbara C. Ewell, "6: *The Awakening*," *Kate Chopin*. New York: Ungar Publishing Co., 1986, pp. 142–45, 149–51, 155, 158. Copyright © 1986 by The Ungar Publishing Co. Reproduced by permission.

For her, uncompromising realism embodied her unique viewpoint: the tale itself reveals its truths. She had, to echo [literary critic and feminist] Elaine Showalter's fine distinction, learned to express the "wild zone" of her own perspective through the conventional restraints of a studied realism. What she had yet to learn—as did Edna—was the outrage with which her simple effort at truth-telling would be greeted.

Chopin Permits No Easy Answers

As in much of her fiction, Chopin's sense of a complex reality permits no easy answers to the moral questions raised by this conflict between the individual and social restraints. Instead, by withholding the moral of this moralistic tale and leaving the nature and value of Edna's awakening essentially unresolved, Chopin delineates the difficulty of calibrating the appropriate relationship between the self and society. The disconcerting ambiguity of the novel's resolutions thus only confounds our expectations of authorial judgment. Having engaged our sympathies by her vivid fiction, Chopin then forces us to appraise them by the harsh light of reality.

The crux around which Chopin fashions this study of the conflict between self and society is the uncertain figure of Edna Pontellier. Like Emma Bovary [heroine of Gustave Flaubert's *Madame Bovary*], the similarity of whose plight is often noted, Edna is incurably romantic, unconsciously sensual, headstrong, indecisive, and an unlikely subject for the self-realization in which the novel engages her. Indeed, an early editorial chapter defines the nature and difficulty of her task with unmistakable wryness:

> In short, Mrs. Pontellier was beginning to realize her position in the universe as a human being, and to recognize her relations as an individual to the world within and about her. This may seem like a ponderous weight of wisdom to descend upon the soul of a young woman of twenty-

eight—perhaps more wisdom than the Holy Ghost is usually pleased to vouchsafe to any woman.

But the beginning of things, of a world especially, is necessarily vague, tangled, chaotic, and exceedingly disturbing.
How few of us ever emerge from such beginning! How many
souls perish in its tumult!

Self-Fulfillment Comes with a Price

Chopin's characteristic irony here underlines both the folly
and the urgency of Edna's need for self-understanding. Edna
must willy-nilly come to terms with herself both as a distinct
individual and in relation to a world "within and about her."
Though Chopin understood clearly enough the universality of
this imperative, she also recognized the peculiar difficulties
faced by women. In her own era, women's roles were well defined—in relation to men—and presumably required no further differentiation. Encouraged to self-sacrifice rather than
self-realization, women like Edna had to overcome tradition
and biology as well as the intransigence of social structures in
any effort at self-assertion. Even an essential reality like sexuality was too often disguised as romance, vaguely mingled
with love.

But while these obstacles are formidable, and include
Edna's personal weaknesses, Chopin faces squarely the consequences of Edna's recognition of "her position in the universe
as a human being." Like her predecessor Adrienne in [Chopin's
short story] "Lilacs," Edna must bear the full brunt of both
her freedom and her understanding, despite the unforeseen
inadequacies limiting them. Fundamental to Edna's self-
awakening is the recognition of her physical being, an awareness several of Chopin's female characters (and some males)
also initially lack, but which constitutes a critical prelude to
consciousness. Promoted by her motherless childhood and
domineering father, Edna's customary reserve disguises a self-
repression that she, like Louise Mallard [in "The Story of an

Hour"], assumes is natural. But the sensual atmosphere of the Gulf, which permeates the novel, and the easygoing openness of Creole culture work to loosen this "mantle of reserve that had always enveloped her," leading Edna to a new awareness of her body and ultimately of the hidden self it expresses.

Though Edna's discovery of her own sensuality culminates in Arobin's embraces, it is implicit early in the novel. Attracted to Adèle, for example, by her "sensuous susceptibility to beauty," Edna responds readily to her friend's sympathetic caresses and unfolds to her with unaccustomed candor the recollections of the past that the "delicious picture" of the sea before them has inspired. Edna's initial childhood memory, which significantly reflects her spiritual condition, is primarily sensory: walking aimlessly through tall, green grasses in the hot summer sun. The unfamiliarity of Edna's physical awareness is also evident at Madame Antoine's where, having undressed for sleep, Edna is acutely conscious, as if "for the first time," of her own flesh. The sensual satisfaction she takes from her nap and from the meal that follows initiates a rhythm of sleeping and eating in the novel, underlining both the physical realities to which Edna is adjusting and the novel's central metaphor. "Awakening" to her own physical being, Edna exults in her concrete individuality. Only later do the real consequences of that awakening become apparent. . . .

Adèle and Reisz Represent Two Roles

Edna's confusion of romance and passion—and the comprehension that the experience of passion brings—is familiar in Chopin's fiction. Convinced of the power of sensuality, Chopin recognized the consequences of its suppression, especially for women. Her concern is echoed in a letter she received after the novel appeared, a letter purportedly from Dr. Dunrobin Thomson, a British physician, but now suspected to have been from an anonymous friend. The writer observed that the frequent confusion of sex and romance by many nineteenth-century women was a consequence of their prudish sexual education. Taught "that passion is disgraceful," respectable women could only label their inevitable sexual urges as "love," and thus became unable to distinguish affection from mere physical attraction. They remained emotional adolescents.

Edna's idealized fantasies of passionate union thus distinctly conflict with the experience she seeks as an individual. In her affair with Arobin, she recognizes the fallacy of her belief that sexuality and love—"her relations as an individual to the world within and about her"—are inseparable. Chopin delineates these irreconcilable desires (for selfhood and relationship) most notably in the characters of Edna's two closest friends, Mlle. Reisz and Adèle Ratignolle.

Held up as a model even by Léonce, Adèle perfectly embodies the social definitions of womanhood. Her marriage epitomizes the ideal "fusion of two human beings into one." Fulfilled by one another, the Ratignolles have submerged themselves in the roles society prescribes for intimacy: for women, that of wife and mother; for men, that of attentive provider. Possessing "every womanly grace and charm," Adèle represents exactly what Edna is not, a mother-woman, the dominant type at Grande Isle:

> It was easy to know them, fluttering about with extended, protecting wings when any harm, real or imaginary, threatened their precious brood. They were women who idolized their children, worshiped their husbands, and esteemed it a holy privilege to efface themselves as individuals and grow wings as ministering angels.

But while Edna recognizes Adèle's "blind contentment" in this role, she sees in it "an appalling and hopeless ennui." Trying to explain herself to her friend, Edna says that she would readily give up the unessential (her money or her life) for her children, but she wouldn't, she insists, "give myself."

But if Edna cannot sacrifice "the essential" for her children, as Adèle evidently can, neither does she possess Mlle.

Reisz's courageous soul. Independent and defiantly unmarried, Mademoiselle is also solitary, with "a disposition to trample on the rights of others." Edna admires the stiff courage of Mademoiselle's unconventionality, but she has neither her daring nor her willingness to live alone and celibate. Edna simply cannot reject the very sensual awareness that has promised her self-possession. . . .

The Need for Selfhood

If Edna's affair with Arobin gives her some control of her sexuality (an expression of individuality), her desire for a more complete relationship with Robert is thwarted. Her "soft, cool, delicate kiss" with its "voluptuous sting" unmistakably manifests her new-found initiative as well as her passionate intents. But Edna cannot fit Robert's reality to her dream of a mutually free, sensuous union. Robert can see Edna only in conventional terms, and he is visibly shocked by her rebuke of his own "wild dream" that Léonce can free her from her obstructing marriage. "I am," she laughingly insists, "no longer one of Mr. Pontellier's possessions to dispose of or not. I give myself, where I choose." Unable to conceive of a woman apart from the conventional garb of wife—or of passion without a saving respectability—Robert quietly leaves, too "honorable" to encumber their love with sex, too traditional to bear the consequences of Edna's new self-possession.

But if Robert's dream of propriety persists, Edna's dream of independence does not. The final limitations of her gender and history soon force themselves upon her in the narrative guise of Adèle's summons to her childbed. Edna and Robert's last *tête-à-tête* is thus tellingly interrupted by an unsubtle reminder of the consequences of the sexuality that Edna is inviting. . . .

Edna's path to integrity then is not a way deliberately chosen. Her ineffectual efforts and ultimate failure to think through her situation reiterate the irrational, emotional forces that have impelled her toward her destiny. With her iconoclasm more fate than will, Edna epitomizes the ambivalences that Chopin's fiction had unflinchingly confronted throughout its course. Edna's desire for integrity, like the familiar patterns and happy endings of local color, has undeniable appeal. But just as life often contradicts those hopeful patterns, so does an intransigent social and physical reality thwart Edna's efforts at selfhood. And having seen the attraction and value of one and the force and obstinacy of the other, Chopin could deny neither. But if Edna's fate implies a pessimistic appraisal of the individual's chances against the world, Chopin also insists on Edna's triumph. Like [some of the characters from Chopin's other works, e.g.,] Mrs. Mallard or Mrs. Summers or Athénaïse, Edna at least knows the possibilities for selfhood, even if reality painfully denies them. . . .

Chopin Addresses Serious Themes

[*The Awakening*] quietly implicates us in its probing of such moral questions as the nature of sexuality, selfhood, and freedom, the meaning of adultery and suicide, and the relationship between biological destiny and personal choice. It is a novel that moves and disturbs us by its confrontation with the sheer obstinacy of our collective and individual humanity. And the subtlety of that confrontation assures *The Awakening* a permanent place in the American literary canon.

Edna's Suicide Is an Act of Freedom

Per Seyersted

Per Seyersted is one of the most influential biographers of Kate Chopin and is generally credited with reviving interest in her and her major work, The Awakening. *With Emily Toth, he collected and edited* Kate Chopin's Private Papers. *He was a professor of American literature at the University of Oslo in Norway.*

The Awakening is an existential novel concerned with whether or not it is possible for a woman in the Victorian age to forge an autonomous existence, suggests Per Seyersted in the following viewpoint. Although she fails to reconcile her desire for freedom with the constraints of society, Edna is ultimately triumphant, he argues. It was impossible for women to be truly independent in a patriarchal society, Seyersted maintains, and Edna acknowledges this bitter truth with her suicide.

[E dna] takes her life because she, on the one hand, insists on sexual and spiritual freedom, and, on the other, acknowledges a duty not to "trample upon the little lives." Her suicide was entirely valid for her time, when her ideas of self-assertion were bound to be condemned outright by the Victorian moral vigilantes. But social conditions were mutable to Kate Chopin, and she never lets her heroine attack them. As if she foresaw that the era would come when the advanced woman would be less branded and her children thus less stigmatized, she included also two aspects of the human condition which she must have seen as destined to plague even the modern Edna.

The Awakening and Women's Issues

Freedom Has a Steep Price

The first of these is the inevitable loss of illusions, particularly the "singular delusion that love is eternal," as Mrs. Chopin expressed it in a story, and the idea that we can see the reality involved in our passions. "Romances serve but to feed the imagination of the young; they add nothing to the sum of truth," she said in another tale, and in a third: "It was the time when the realities of life clothe themselves in the garb of romance, when Nature's decoys are abroad; when the tempting bait is set." In response to Dr. Mandelet's even more outspoken statements, Mrs. Pontellier remarks: "Yes. . . . To wake up and find—oh! well! perhaps it is better to wake up after all, even to suffer, rather than to remain a dupe to illusions all one's life." What pains Edna is her realization that the idea of the great passion with its lofty, personal attachment, its oneness with the beloved is largely a fiction, a euphemistic disguise for a basically sexual attraction, an animalistic, impersonal drive. "To-day it is Arobin; to-morrow it will be some one else. It makes no difference to me," she thinks as she walks into the water, and in spite of the love she feels for Robert, she foresees that one day he, too, "would melt out of her existence, leaving her alone."

It was perhaps no accident that of the eight [Guy de] Maupassant stories which Kate Chopin translated [from French], one is called "Solitude" and another "Suicide," and that these two tell us that "We are the everlasting playthings of . . . illusions" and that we are always alone, ironically more so when contact with the opposite sex momentarily makes us forget our solitude. Edna realizes the emptiness in sex-rotation, and she sees herself as driven by sovereign sexuality and selfishness, forces which make for loneliness.

As appears from Mrs. Chopin's notebook, she originally titled her novel "A Solitary Soul." When she did this she was no doubt referring in part to Edna's awakening to the loneliness of imperative sexuality, of illusory, evanescent love. But the term refers even more to another aspect of the human condition: the curse of freedom. Kate Chopin's view of life was to a large extent independent of such important currents of thought as idealism, socio-economic determinism, and even religion. The attitude she lets Mrs. Pontellier illustrate comes close to that of existentialism. She seems to say that Edna has a real existence only when she gives her own laws, when she through conscious choice becomes her own creation with an autonomous self. But while such a developmental freedom may strengthen the self, it is accompanied by a growing sense of isolation and aloneness, and also anguish. To realize existence as an authentic subject demands a painful choosing, and man is tempted to run away from it as he—in [existentialist Jean-Paul] Sartre's term—feels "condemned to be free."

Freedom Is Harder for Women

If the process of existential individuation is taxing on a man and freedom a lonely and threatening thing to him, it is doubly so for a woman who attempts to emancipate herself from the state of immanence to which our patriarchal world has assigned her for millenniums. Feminism was well advanced in Kate Chopin's America, and she probably foresaw that woman would obtain the degree of equality with man that she has today. But she could also see that what women mostly demanded, and men only bit by bit granted, was a technical equality which did not alter the basic roles and attitudes of either sex.

She seems to have realized that in the patriarchy, man would not willingly relinquish the role of the conqueror, nor woman that of the conquered. To her, man's instinct of mastery, and the "constant rebuff" which a man feels if a woman lacks "the coquettish, the captivating, the feminine," as she expressed it in a story, were enduring realities. Adèle captivates men by being coquettish and naive and by acting the role of the weak, while Edna is incapable of using her friend's "feline or feminine wiles" or "kittenish display" to attract their notice. Kate Chopin could see how even George Sand's *Indiana* [*Indiana* was the first novel of French writer Amantine Aurore Lucile Dupin, who wrote under the name George Sand], for example, stresses that she is "only a weak woman," and she may have guessed that also her creator, in spite of all her militancy, somewhere deep down subscribed to the myth of the strong man and the weak woman. Had Mérimée loved me, Mme. Sand wrote in a letter after an expected affair with him had failed to get started, "he would have dominated me, and if I had found a man capable of dominating me, I should have been saved, for liberty is eating my life away, and killing me."

The French pioneer here touches the fundamental problem confronting the female emancipationist. As long as girls play with dolls and boys with guns; as long as men dominate and women submit and the Madonna is the chief Christian ideal of a feminine being, society will show a quite compact resistance against woman leaving her traditional role as the weaker sex; consequently, the female feels a tremendous pressure to prove that she is a woman first and only secondly an individual.

The old role is of course in many ways convenient for the woman; she is materially provided for, and also metaphysically—as [French philosopher] Simone de Beauvoir has emphasized—in the sense that she does not need to justify her existence as a wife and mother and that she can largely leave the responsibility for her fate to the man. But the moment she feels it more important to be an individual than to be a woman (or at least a mother-woman), as Edna does, she is in deep water: Unassisted, she has to create her own role and status and define her aims; she must fight society's opposition as well as her own feelings of insecurity and guilt, and—more than a man—she suffers under the liberty in which she must justify her existence. When a woman in the existential manner assumes sole responsibility for her life, which then depends on her own efforts, freedom becomes something of a negative condition and she herself indeed a solitary soul.

Kate Chopin was undoubtedly familiar with the existence of the matriarchies of old and of her own day, and thus aware that the patriarchy was no law of nature. Even so, she seems to see no happy end to woman's quest for freedom. Edna wants to decide over her own life, but this urge brings her despair rather than happiness. She appears to need all her strength to want freedom *from* rather than freedom *to*, and to be too weak both to break the chains and to justify her non-conformist existence through positive performance. The note of pessimism which runs through the book may be due in part to the romantic syndrome which Edna mirrors in her passion, her anguish, and her occasional passivity and desire for nothingness. The ultimate reason for the heroine's feeling of hopelessness, however, is her urge for spiritual emancipation which is so strong that there is no turning back for her: "She did not look back now, but went on and on."

Edna's Suicide Is an Act of Freedom

Edna is defeated in the sense that she cannot meaningfully relate herself to the people around her and in some way integrate her demands with those of society, a society, to be sure, which is responsible for the fact that emancipation is her goal rather than her birthright. Not attempting to come to terms with her selfish drives, she is unable to reach that harmony, that feeling of creative cooperation and companionship with the people around her at which Athénaïse apparently arrives. Yet she is not defeated like Emma Bovary [the heroine of Gustave Flaubert's *Madame Bovary*]: Her death is not so much a result of outer forces crowding her in as a triumphant assertion of her inner liberty.

Mrs. Chopin's heroine does not try to "escape from freedom," to use [psychoanalyst] Erich Fromm's term. Rather, her suicide is the crowning glory of her development from the bewilderment which accompanied her early emancipation to the clarity with which she understands her own nature and the possibilities of her life as she decides to end it. Edna's victory lies in her awakening to an independence that includes an act of renunciation. The novel is something of a landmark in nineteenth-century American literature in that it reaches out beyond woman's obtaining equality in law and love to the existentialist demand for dictating one's own destiny, and even beyond that to the horror of freedom, the immutable affliction for both the women and men who venture that far. What is most important, however, is that the book is a great artistic achievement.

Suicide Was Edna's Only Authentic Choice

Deborah S. Gentry

Deborah S. Gentry is an associate professor in the English Department at Middle Tennessee State University.

Many critics fail to understand the significance of Edna's suicide in The Awakening, *contends Deborah S. Gentry in the following viewpoint. Edna's suicide is heroic, Gentry argues. Gentry concludes that Edna, recognizing that there is no role available to a Victorian woman that permits freedom, makes the only moral choice for a woman who insists on her selfhood.*

The rediscovery of [Kate] Chopin's work and its subsequent legitimization by the critical establishment in the Sixties was quickly followed by her canonization by feminist literary critics in the Seventies. Although it is tempting to see Chopin as a conscious forerunner of the recent feminist movement, [Margaret] Culley points out that Chopin "was never a feminist or a suffragist; in fact, she was suspicious of any ideology. She was committed to personal freedom." What made her fiction appeal to feminists is that she acted out her call for personal freedom from limitations primarily through woman characters, some of the least free members of society. Culley concludes:

> Though Kate Chopin was not a feminist, and *The Awakening* is not a political novel in the narrow sense of the term, it is important to understand the political and social context in which it appeared. A novel exploring the consequences of

Deborah S. Gentry, "Kate Chopin's Rebel with a Cause: Edna Pontellier in *The Awakening*," in *The Art of Dying: Suicide in the Works of Kate Chopin and Sylvia Plath*. New York: Peter Lang Publishing, Inc., 2006, pp. 20–24, 44–45. Copyright © 2006 by Peter Lang Publishing, Inc. Reproduced by permission.

personal—particularly sexual—freedom for the married woman, appearing as it did in a decade much preoccupied with the New Woman in its midst, was certain to provoke strong reactions.

Critics Failed to Understand Edna's Suicide

Another strong contributor to these negative reactions was the novel's ending, Edna Pontellier's suicide, which pleased neither the conservatives of the 1890s nor the liberals of the 2000s, because the former did not see Edna's death as penitent but defiant and the latter do not see it as necessary at all. In fact, Edna's suicide has become a touchstone for the novel's critical analysis. Culley classifies the ending as one of the novel's major problems, and several modern critics see the ending as totally betraying Chopin's characterization of Edna as a strong-willed woman. Ultimately, to make sense of the book, the reader must understand the complex motivations behind Edna's suicide and how the actions of the novel lead inexorably to that conclusion. . . .

Chopin's view of the significance of sexuality in *The Awakening* is not very different from that presented by Ernest Hemingway in *The Sun Also Rises*. At the center of that novel is the character Jake Barnes, whom Hemingway portrays as sexually impotent due to a wound received during the First World War. On the surface, Jake's impotency appears to keep him and Brett Ashley from marrying and presumably living happily ever after. However, by the conclusion of *The Sun Also Rises*, it is clear to the reader that Jake's wound is only an outward symbol of the sterility and absurdity of modern life. *The Sun Also Rises* does not conclude with Jake and Brett killing themselves as Edna does in *The Awakening*, but the tone and theme of the two novels are very similar. Yet critics do not propose that if Jake were suddenly potent again, all of his problems would be resolved, and it is just as ludicrous to presume that sex alone can resolve Edna's problems.

Critics such [Harold] Bloom, [George] Spangler, and [Kenneth] Eble fail to understand the full nature of Edna's awakening, which is nothing short of an awakening to the true circumstances of existence for a woman shorn of the romantic illusions that society foists upon her—an existence in which the deck is so stacked against women that the only true choice left to them is to continue this oppressive existence or to die. Larzer Ziff rightly concludes that "Edna Pontellier is trapped between her illusions and the conditions which society arbitrarily establishes to maintain itself, and she is made to pay." In the context of Chopin's novel, suicide is not a running away from life but a running to it. It becomes the only choice available to a woman who has placed individual dignity and integrity above all else.

Although Bloom states that feminist critics "weakly misread the book" because "it is anything but feminist in its stance," feminist literary critics find that Chopin creates a sympathetic character in Edna Pontellier and that the novel involves us in Edna's struggle—a struggle to find personal freedom and fulfillment in a social structure that demands female submission. That this struggle is doomed should not come as a surprise to the reader, since from the first chapter Chopin consistently foreshadows Edna's inevitable failure and death. While it is true that a central point of interest in the book is Edna's relationships with men, Chopin's focus is not primarily on Edna as a sexually unfulfilled person or as a woman subsequently fulfilled by her sexual relationship with Alcee Arobin. In other words, sex is not at the center of Edna's quest. Rather, this quest is established from the outset as being grounded in the Romantic ideal, the need of the individual ego to assert itself without restraint. In this regard, Bloom sees Chopin as a daughter of [poet] Walt Whitman. He states:

Walt Whitman, one of the roughs, an American, the self of *Song of Myself,* lusts after "the real me" or "me myself" of Walt Whitman. Chopin's heroine, Edna, becomes, as it were, one of the roughs, an American, when she allows herself to lust after her real me, her me myself ... Edna, like Walt, falls in love with her own body, and her infatuation with the inadequate Robert is merely a screen for her overwhelming obsession, which is to nurse and mother herself.

Notice Bloom's reference to the need for feminine ministration and validation at the end of this quotation. This need is at the heart of both Edna's and thus the novel's struggle because women have societal and biological limits that prevent them from fulfilling their romantic egos.

Women Are Reduced by Men

Traditionally, the male romantic ego has received external validation through women. It is through their conquest of women that men have seen themselves as freed from the restraints inherent in their humanity. As Camille Paglia states in *Sexual Personae*, "Women have borne the symbolic burden of man's imperfections, his grounding in nature." She adds, "Man, repelled by his debt to a physical mother, created an alternate reality, a heterocosm to give him the illusion of freedom." Thus man has constructed civilization for the purpose of distancing nature and reducing its ability to limit him. In this process, he has constructed a sexist and racist system designed to place him in a position of superiority over women and over other men, who can be designated as flawed, subhuman, or alien. As Virginia Woolf states in *A Room of One's Own*, "Women have served all these centuries as looking-glasses possessing the magic and delicious power of reflecting the figure of man at twice its natural size. Without that power probably the earth would still be swamp and jungle." This power creates for dominant males a sense of superiority and entitlement not just in relationship to the objects of their oppression, but to nature and its power as well. This does not mean that the man actually has power over the arbitrariness and ne-

American poet Walt Whitman (1819–1892). Deborah S. Gentry refutes literary critic Harold Bloom's claim that Kate Chopin can be seen as an heir of Whitman's individualist style. AP Images.

gation of death, but only that he feels that he does and he feels a sense of entitlement and invulnerability. So, for example, a man does not see himself as growing old; what he sees is his wife growing old, and he feels a sense of outrage at her for this betrayal of him. Rather than confront his personal mortality, he simply gets a new, younger wife. In some respects, this enormous sense of ego lies at the heart of the romantic ideal. But for this ideal to function, it needs a sense of entitlement and a way of projecting nature into an opponent he can grapple with.

In order to accomplish this, man has projected nature onto woman and subjugated it in his subjugation of her. However, it becomes very difficult for this philosophical construct to function as intended if it is a woman who is obsessed with the Romantic ideal. Paglia contends:

> Woman does not dream of transcendental or historical escape from natural cycle, since she is that cycle . . . The more woman aims for personal identity and autonomy, the more she develops her imagination, the fiercer will be her struggle with nature—that is with the intractable laws of her own body.

And this conflict is at the intuitive heart of Chopin's novel and Edna's dilemma. This is why Chopin is not Walt Whitman's daughter as Harold Bloom insists. In the America of the 1890s, she is instead Whitman's wife, experiencing the futility and absurdity of the Romantic ideal. As we shall see later, Edna does not defy nature, but rather is identified with it. Although there is nothing new in identifying women characters in literature with nature, this identification means something very different to Chopin, since she is a woman. . . .

That Edna's suicide is misunderstood by some critics is not surprising, considering the hold the romantic paradigm has on the literary depiction of female suicide. In *The Awakening*, Chopin remasculinizes female suicide. Contrary to the conclusions of critics such as George Spangler who feel that the ending does not fit the novel, there is much textual evidence foreshadowing Edna's suicide. Spangler makes his the standard case in "*The Awakening*: A Partial Dissent," stating, ". . . one can easily and happily join in the praise that in recent years has been given to *The Awakening*—one can, that is, until one reaches the conclusion of the novel, which is unsatisfactory because it is fundamentally evasive." Spangler elaborates on what he sees as the problem:

> And what is wrong with this conclusion? Its great fault is inconsistent characterization, which asks the reader to accept a different and diminished Edna from the one developed so impressively before. Throughout the novel the most striking feature of Edna's character has been her strength of will, her ruthless determination to get her own way . . . Yet in the final pages, Mrs. Chopin asks her reader to believe in an Edna who is completely defeated by the loss of Robert, to believe in the paradox of a woman who has awakened to passional life and yet quietly, almost thoughtlessly, chooses death.

Thus Spangler sees Edna as defeated and destroyed by *mal d'amour* [lovesickness], but he has missed the consistency of symbols and tone throughout the novel that predicts the ending, such as the parallel swimming scenes and the images of the sea at both the beginning and end of the novel. Ultimately, [Sandra] Gilbert and [Susan] Gubar's general feminist approach [in *The Madwoman in the Attic*] is more rewarding. Edna awakens to her situation as a woman, and in her quest for identity through a life of significant action, she must paradoxically choose suicide as the only means available to her to achieve her goal. As Larzer Ziff concludes in *The American 1890s. Life and Times of a Lost Generation* concerning Chopin's message in writing the novel:

> Whether girls should be educated free of illusions, if possible, whether society should change the conditions it imposes on women, or whether both are needed, the author does not say; the novel is about what happened to Edna Pontellier.

And in this novel, Edna writes her story with her body.

The Awakening Is Concerned with Personal Rather than Social Issues

Elizabeth Fox-Genovese

Elizabeth Fox-Genovese was an American historian who wrote about women in the antebellum American South. For a number of years, she was a professor of humanities at Emory University, where she was founder of the Institute for Women's Studies.

To fully appreciate the complexities of The Awakening, *it is important to place the novel in the context of the antebellum South, Elizabeth Fox-Genovese contends in the following selection. At the time that Chopin was writing, a number of white, upper-class, southern women were agitating for women's rights, including the right to vote. The issues they were addressing were concerned with gender, race, and class and can be categorized as social problems, Fox-Genovese asserts. Chopin appeared to have little interest in social problems, according to the author. Her concerns were more personal, having to do with female sexuality, a fundamental part of a woman's nature.*

Kate Chopin, on her own accounting, had scant interest in "social problems." She did not, for example, last long as a member of St. Louis's Wednesday Club, in which worthy matrons met to promote their intellectual improvement and the welfare of their city's poor. Yet *The Awakening* has, at least in part, earned its new-found place in our canon since it purportedly addresses a social problem: the condition of women. The possible disjuncture between Chopin's intentions and the

Elizabeth Fox-Genovese, "*The Awakening* in the Context of the Experience, Culture, and Values of Southern Women," in *Approaches to Teaching Chopin's "The Awakening,"* Bernard Koloski, ed. New York: Modern Language Association of America, 1988, pp. 34–39. Copyright © 1988 by the Modern Language Association of America. Reproduced by permission.

perspective of her modern readers, especially the female ones, challenges those of us who wish to teach the novel with some attention to historical context.

Not a Social Problem Novel

There seems little doubt, to take the obvious comparison, that we can legitimately teach Charlotte Gilman's "The Yellow Wallpaper"—whatever its intrinsic merits—as a tract against the constraints of the "patriarchal" institution of marriage. The legitimacy of so teaching *The Awakening* remains far more questionable. Yet most critics, however divergent their specific readings, implicitly treat *The Awakening* as a problem novel that cries out for a "solution." Chopin's distinctive style and structure—her mode of composition and her literary strategy—fashioned this destiny for her text. For the novel follows the pattern of her own short stories, visibly influenced by [Guy de] Maupassant, in suggesting that the ending reveals the meaning of the text. This strategy invites readers of *The Awakening*, to look to Edna's suicide as the key to the preceding account of a brief period in her life. Edna's suicide in sum, represents a complex—one is tempted to say overdetermined—judgment on the society and institutions that have forced Edna to commit the act, or perhaps a judgment on Edna herself.

Chopin's explicit discussion of women's sexuality establishes the visible point of conflict between her heroine and society, as it also establishes the point of conflict between Chopin and the dominant mores of her day. American culture in the late 1890s was not ready for an open assault on women's social identification with marriage, or even for an open defense of women's sexual and sensual individualism. The social and personal questions apparently merge in Edna's "awakening" to sexuality, which Chopin identifies with her protagonist's "beginning to realize her position in the universe as a human being, and to recognize her relations as an individual to the world within and about her." Yet Chopin's own diction makes the nice and necessary distinction that I find fruitful in teaching the novel in historical context. For Chopin's words differentiate between the realization of self as a human being (a private and psychological matter) and the recognition of one's relations as an individual to others (a public or social matter).

The Awakening shocked Chopin's contemporaries for the same reason that it has earned the admiration of recent generations: it candidly acknowledges women's sexual impulses. Modern readers, especially students, tend to view Edna's awakening to her sexuality as logically portending her struggle for liberation. Yet Chopin remains more ambiguous, thus inviting multiple, even contradictory, readings. Nonetheless, close attention to *The Awakening*'s historical context helps to clarify Chopin's probable views and, even more, to recapture the discourses and social expectations within which they unfolded.

Marriage Objectifies Women

It would be difficult to argue that Chopin intended *The Awakening* to be primarily a polemic against marriage as a social institution, or even primarily a polemic against the social limitations on women's relations as individuals to others. Yet Chopin does hint that late-nineteenth-century marriages cast women as the objects of others rather than as the free subjects of their own fates. Thus she introduces Edna through her husband's gaze and, in a frequently cited line, allows that he regarded her as a "valuable piece of personal property which has suffered some damage." This view of marriage permits us to link *The Awakening* to the growing public complaints of some American women against the subordination of women to men within marriage. Yet Chopin, unlike an Elizabeth Cady Stanton or a Charlotte Perkins Gilman [American social reformers], does not let the question rest there. Having allowed for the social dimension, she rapidly reveals the multiple possibilities for happiness and shared understanding between

American author Charlotte Perkins Gilman (1860–1935), whose semiautobiographical short story "The Yellow Wallpaper" (1892) is considered a foundational work of feminist litera-ture for its critique of marriage. Fotosearch/Getty Images.

husbands and wives, including Edna and Léonce. Since Chopin's Edna invites comparison with [Henrik] Ibsen's Nora [protagonist of *A Doll's House*], it is worth recalling Chopin's scornful dismissal of Ibsen's work as too deeply hostage to specific, transitory social conditions:

> Human impulses do not change and can not so long as men and women continue to stand in the relation to one another which they have occupied since our knowledge of their existence began. It is why [ancient Greek tragedian] Aeschylus is true, and [playwright William] Shakespeare is true to-day, and why Ibsen will not be true in some remote tomorrow, however forcible and representative he may be for the hour, because he takes for his themes social problems which by their very nature are mutable.

In fact, Ibsen's depiction of the ways in which marriage imprisoned women and stunted their development more closely resembled the concerns of northern than of southern women. The differences are subtle, but worth attention. The driving force of the women's movement, narrowly understood as the movement to improve women's social position or rights, came out of the Northeast and its offshoots, the Old Northwest and the Western Reserve, where the movement had been closely and explicitly tied to the antislavery movement. In the 1850s, the gifted proslavery and antifeminist polemicist Louisa S. McCord had mercilessly castigated the advocates of women's rights as would-be topplers of all social order worthy of the name. McCord never doubted women's capacities; she merely deplored the self-indulgent and irresponsible attempt to see those capacities as identical to men's or to extrapolate from them egalitarian social principles. In substance, she agreed with the radical northern analysis: the social position of women was inextricably linked to what she called "the social question." But whereas northern reformers saw the link as justification for change in both gender and social relations, she saw it as proof that women must accept the roles that their physical weakness and social arrangements had allotted to them.

An Age of Feminist Awareness

By the period of the Gilded Age, during which Chopin wrote, some southern women of her class were becoming committed to various kinds of social reform, including that of their own social and political status. Nonetheless, their efforts on behalf of women's rights, especially the right to suffrage, remained as firmly bound as ever to the social question—which, in the postreconstruction South, meant the race question. Although southern women differed in the conclusions they drew from the necessary connection between gender relations and race and class relations, they agreed—and how could they not?—on the force of the connection. Chopin appears to have avoided taking a stand on the relations between what she called women's "independence" and women's social and political rights, much less on the relations between women's independence and race and class relations in general. That silence provides an important caution against any simple social interpretation of *The Awakening*. Does Chopin, in other words, give any indication that she intends her novel as an intervention in the narrow institutional discussion of women's rights?

The legacy of antebellum slave society, and especially of the war that destroyed that society, weighed heavily on southern women of Chopin's generation. Few had not lost kin or suffered reversals of fortune. Most, like [Louisiana author] Grace King and Chopin herself, had fathers, uncles, or grandfathers who fought in the war, and they also had their own memories of confrontations with, or flights from, federal troops. The ensuing period of reconstruction left its special scars—personal, financial, and political. For Chopin, her years on her husband's plantations in Natchitoches Parish must have been like a return to the ancien régime [the former order], albeit a return sprinkled with bitter reminders of that régime's passing. Perhaps above all, for the women of Chopin's class, race, and generation, the late antebellum years harbored formative childhood memories. In their early teens during the collapse of southern slave society, they had been being reared to take their places as ladies in that society, following the tradition of the mothers, grandmothers, even great grandmothers who provided their most important models. For such women, the special legacy of slavery's passing lay in their having the responsibility as women to help to preserve the closest possible facsimile of antebellum class and race relations, especially if they or their families had suffered reversals of fortune.

Perhaps never more than during the postwar decades, white womanhood stood as the bulwark against social and racial chaos. The burden must have been heavy, as [novelist] Ellen Glasgow, in the succeeding generation, would suggest. But for many southern women, committed as they were to the values of their class and race, it also had its compensations. In any event, it is difficult to find any systematic rebellion against women's prescribed role in the writings of the first postbellum generations of women writers. Not that those writings lack their share of strong, resourceful, and even, to use Chopin's word, independent women. They simply lack women who challenge the social order in the name of women's individual rights.

Gender Differs from Sexuality

This argument may seem a strange one to advance as a possible guide to teaching *The Awakening* in historical context, but it does provide precisely such a context however one ultimately interprets Chopin's position as manifest in Edna. More, it provides a fruitful perspective from which to encourage students to articulate their own responses. In this respect, I have found it useful to encourage students to distinguish between gender and sexuality in assessing Chopin's notion of female independence. The distinction inevitably remains messy, but withal heuristically helpful. For gender can be presented as the social construction of sexuality, and sexuality itself as a dimension of women's private, biologically rooted identity. Gender roles, in this context, consist in what we might call society's views or expectations of women: daughter, wife, mother, nurturer, lady. Gender roles remain deeply hostage to considerations of class and race. Sexuality, in contrast, refers to women's nature or essence, to what women share across class and racial lines, to the eternal woman.

Complications in the application of this distinction arise because different cultures treat the relations between gender and sexuality differently. With respect to the examples at hand, northern middle-class culture tended to present gender and sexuality as isomorphic [in a similar form]. For a northern woman to revolt against her sexual suppression was to call into question her gender role. For a northern woman to challenge the constraints on her gender was, in her community's view if not always in her own, implicitly to assert her sexuality. The egalitarian ideals of northern democracy—republicanism to be precise—imposed the association of gender and sexuality. The private feelings and behavior of middle-class women had implications for the behavior of all women, who, at least in ideology, were assumed to resemble them in both gender and sexual attributes.

Southern culture had traditionally viewed the question differently. To be sure, southern society placed as high a premium on female chastity (some might say a higher one) as did northern society—and for social and racial reasons. The sexuality of upper-class white women—like its reverse, their chastity—constituted the visible and sacred prize of upper-class white men, who were honor-bound to defend it. But this very claim also reveals the defense of white female sexuality to have been a class and racial, rather than an individual, matter.

Life in the postbellum South intensified the explicit identification of the tight relations between gender, class, and race
relations. Southern suffragists varied in degree, but not in
substance, on their analysis of the necessary link between
women's rights and the racial balance of their society: they
concurred that the woman's vote should not be allowed to increase the black vote. Chopin did not participate in the heated
discussions about women's rights, which she surely viewed as
yet another side of the social question. But aspects of her
work strongly suggest that she sought, as it were, to write
around or above the issue. Neither *The Awakening* nor any of
her other writings suggest that she secretly espoused woman
suffrage or related causes. To the contrary, everything that she
wrote, including *The Awakening*, indicates that she viewed
women's independence as a personal more than a social matter. In one moving passage, she does imply that her own independence derived in no small measure from the deaths of her
husband and her mother—that is, from her release from social constraints as embodied in those she loved. Passages in
The Awakening even suggest that she recognized children as a
possible fetter on women's self-determination, although she
never otherwise hinted that she felt so about her own. But the
constant, underlying current in her writings makes it clear
that she took no inconsiderable pride in having attained a sophisticated and independent maturity on her own, within the
limitations that her society imposed. In *The Awakening*, she
carefully delineates both the possibility for women's happiness
within marriage (Mme Ratignolle) and the possibility for their
independence from it (Mlle Reisz).

A Tragic View of the Human Condition

Strange as it may seem to modern readers, there is reason to
believe that Chopin intended her explorations of women's
sexual self-awareness to pose less of a threat to the social order of her world than explorations of their social indepen-

dence would have. In this respect, her attitudes represent a stark reversal of those of Gilman, as manifested in the two women's attitudes toward doctors. For Gilman, the doctor constituted a kind of political vanguard and buttress of the husband, understood as oppressor. For Chopin, he constituted a wise confidant who fully appreciated the complexities of woman's nature. Chopin's open discussion of women's sexuality proved, in the event, to shock her southern contemporaries as profoundly as her northern ones. The South, after all, remained too American. Even the veneer of New Orleans local color—and all southerners accepted New Orleans as different—and of Chopin's self-conscious European style did not protect her. Chopin may not fully, or more to the point consciously, have known what she was risking, but she did know what she was attempting.

Chopin's sympathy for women's personal and sexual independence sank its roots in a tragic view of the human condition derived from a Catholic sensibility that persisted long after Chopin had abandoned regular Catholic practice. This view of human nature resulted in the notion that personal matters should be personal, should not challenge the social order. Chopin's preoccupation with European naturalism only reinforced her inherited sense of how original sin and established social relations pressed on the individual's internal and external possibilities for freedom. Edna ultimately fails in her bid for freedom because she lacked the personal strength to realize her nature within the possibilities afforded by her society, because she failed to recognize the difference between the contingent and the essential. Chopin gambled on presenting woman's nature as a universal problem. She set her sights on Aeschylus and Shakespeare, not on Ibsen. She may have thought that her attempt to treat sexuality independent of gender relations respected the social values of southern society, but she misjudged.

In *The Awakening*, Kate Chopin self-consciously sought to move beyond the specific southern identification of her local-color stories. She surely did not intend her novel as a specific reflection of the values of southern women, parochially defined. Yet today, the novel gains resonance if read and taught in historical context. As a novelist, Chopin navigated between specificity of detail and universality of theme. It is difficult not to wonder if she fully understood how firmly that strategy linked her to the emerging modern tradition of southern letters. No social or domestic novelist, she wrote of the female human condition as a full member of that distinctive culture which would also inform the work of [southern authors] William Alexander Percy and William Faulkner.

Three Women in *The Awakening* Portray Different Roles for Women

Peggy Skaggs

Peggy Skaggs taught at Angelo State University in Texas.

Of the three major women characters in The Awakening, *Edna comes closest to fulfilling her potential, Peggy Skaggs argues in the following viewpoint. Settling for a maternal role, Adéle is subsumed by the needs of others. Dedicating herself to the role of artist, Mademoiselle Reisz cuts herself off from relationships with others. In Skaggs's view, Edna rebels against the role of women in her society by asserting both her independence and her sexuality. Thwarted in her attempt to have a full existence, Skaggs maintains, Edna determines that no existence is better than living a half-life and takes her own life.*

Three important female characters—Adèle Ratignolle, Mademoiselle Reisz, and Edna Pontellier—appear in *The Awakening*, but not one achieves her full potential as a human being: Adèle settles more or less happily for a partial existence as "mother-woman"; Mademoiselle Reisz settles more or less miserably for a partial existence as artist; only Edna refuses to settle for less than full development as a person, and her desperate search for fulfillment hurtles toward failure from its inception to its tragic finale. Edna's search encounters most of the contradictory forces Chopin marked throughout her earlier work as operating against women as they seek to fulfill the basic human needs for love, place, and autonomy—the emotional satisfactions the author believes are requisite to a fully realized human life. . . .

Edna, however, is truly a tragic heroine. More honest in her self-awareness than Adèle, more dependent upon human relationships than Mademoiselle Reisz, Edna will not settle for living as less than a complete person; but forces beyond her control doom inexorably her search for a full, meaningful, and satisfying individuality.

"Awakening" to Life

One critic has called Edna's "awakening" purely sexual; another has called it sexual and "spiritual"; still another has described it as a sexual awakening that is "a metaphoric expression of multitudinous awakenings of deeper and still more powerful emotional forces than the relatively uncomplex feeling of aroused passion." Surely, her awakening encompasses more than physical passion since it begins well before her sexual feelings start to stir.

Quietly, Edna's awakening begins merely with a growing awareness of the inadequacy of her existence. She awakens first to a sense of vague dissatisfaction, next to the aesthetic joy of music, and then to the physical pleasure of swimming. Only after this point in the story does she begin to feel a strong sexual attraction toward Robert, and her full sexual awakening does not occur until months later. Edna's sexual awakening, then, follows her awakening to her own individuality, rather than the other way around. In fact, Chopin may well have intended to illustrate that a woman cannot fully respond sexually until she has first achieved some sense of autonomy. . . .

Edna's Marriage Disintegrates

Once Edna's consciousness of herself as an individual has begun to stir, her relationship with Léonce can do nothing but deteriorate. Although he believes he loves his wife, although he is a kind and generous man, although he seeks and follows the best advice he can get in his marital confusion, Léonce's immersion in the culture that idolizes the "mother-woman" precludes his ever understanding his wife's awakening need for autonomy. If that awakening were primarily sexual, Léonce might have come to understand it; indeed, it might well have improved their marriage. But all the thought patterns of his forty years, his entire way of looking at life, blind him to the fact that a woman may properly have a "position in the universe as a human being" apart from her place as wife and mother. . . .

Edna Awakens Sexually

Stirred by her newly emerging need to be recognized as a person, Edna turns to Robert, who has chosen her as the object of the innocent but flattering attention he each year devotes to one of the married women at his mother's resort. The Creole women he has so honored during previous summers have never taken his attentions seriously; but Edna, enmeshed in forces beyond her comprehension, let alone control, begins to depend upon his understanding presence. For instance, when walking with her husband and the Ratignolles, she hears Robert's voice behind them and wonders why he does not join them: "It was unlike him not to. Of late he had sometimes held away from her for an entire day, redoubling his devotion upon the next and the next, as though to make up for hours that had been lost. She missed him the days when some pretext served to take him away from her, just as one misses the sun on a cloudy day without having thought much about the sun when it was shining." At the end of the day they spend together on the island, following the Pontelliers' quarrel about Edna's not coming to bed at Léonce's command, Robert leaves Edna waiting for her husband to return from Klein's hotel. Edna wonders why: "It did not occur to her to think he might have grown tired of being with her the livelong day. She was not tired, and she felt that he was not. She regretted that he had gone. It was so much more natural to have him stay."

But Edna herself realizes that sexual desire strongly colors her affection for Robert only when he suddenly announces that he is going to Mexico. After he tells her good-bye,

> Edna bit her handkerchief convulsively, striving to hold back and to hide, even from herself as she would have hidden from another, the emotion which was troubling—tearing— her. Her eyes were brimming with tears. . . .

> For the first time she recognized anew the symptoms of infatuation which she had felt incipiently as a child, as a girl in her earliest teens, and later as a young woman.

After he leaves, she feels that his going "had some way taken the brightness, the color, the meaning out of everything. The conditions of her life were in no way changed, but her whole existence was dulled, like a faded garment which seems to be no longer worth wearing." And as her personality emerges during his absence, her passion for him grows apace.

By the time Robert returns from Mexico, Edna has fully emerged from among Léonce's possessions, and she greets him with frank and open joy. He responds, "Mrs. Pontellier, you are cruel." The same Creole, Catholic culture that produced Léonce also shaped Robert, and he understands Edna no better than her husband does. At first Robert avoids her, and then he confesses that he dreams of asking Léonce to set her free to marry him. Her response shocks him deeply:

> "You have been a very, very foolish boy, wasting your time dreaming of impossible things when you speak of Mr. Pontellier setting me free! I am no longer one of Mr. Pontellier's possessions to dispose of or not. I give myself where I choose. If he were to say, 'Here, Robert, take her and be happy; she is yours,' I should laugh at you both."

> His face grew a little white. "What do you mean?" he asked.

But before Edna can try to explain, a messenger comes to take her to Adèle.

Edna Discovers Her Individuality

Upon returning from Adèle's accouchement [confinement to bed during childbirth], Edna finds only a note from Robert, informing her that he has left—because he loves her. Thus, Edna learns that her imagination alone has endowed Robert with sympathetic understanding, that he comprehends no better than Léonce her need to be recognized as an individual human being, a person as well as a woman. Now she realizes that, inasmuch as he too sees her only as female, not as a whole person, "the day would come when he, too, and the thought of him would melt out of her existence, leaving her alone." And finally, as Edna gives herself at last to the sea, she recalls Robert's last message, thinking "'Good-by—because I love you.' He did not know; he did not understand. He would never understand."

An emphatic surge in Edna's sexual feelings accompanies her developing autonomy. Unable to satisfy this newly felt sexual need through her husband, whose possessiveness is responsible for its earlier repression, and equally unable to satisfy it through Robert because he is an honorable man who flees to Mexico, Edna "gives herself where she chooses"—to Alcée Arobin. An attractive man, Alcée "possessed a good figure, a pleasing face, not overburdened with depth of thought or feeling; and his dress was that of the conventional man of fashion," but Edna recognizes the purely sexual nature of his attraction: "the effrontery in his eyes repelled the old, vanishing self in her, yet drew all her awakening sensuousness." Perhaps a paradox of woman's nature makes her incapable of a fully awakened "sensuousness" (Chopin's euphemism for sexual responsiveness) unless she has some sense of power over her own responses; but such a fully awakened "sensuousness" then urges her to surrender the very autonomy that has made it possible. At any rate, Edna knows well before the event that she will "give herself," at least her body, to Alcée. But she knows too that "Alcée Arobin was absolutely nothing to her."

On the evening after Edna learns that Robert is coming home, Alcée senses that the time has arrived to consummate the seduction. He kisses her: "It was the first kiss of her life to which her nature had really responded. It was a flaming torch that kindled desire." Then Chopin includes another of the brief, staccato chapters that she uses much like exclamation points in *The Awakening*. Only fourteen lines long, even shorter than the chapter that describes Edna's dawning awareness of herself as an individual human being, this one describes her ambiguous, but honest and powerful, reactions following her first sexual fulfillment:

> Edna cried a little that night after Arobin left her. It was only one phase of the multitudinous emotions which had assailed her. . . . There was her husband's reproach looking at her from the external things . . . which he had provided for her external existence. There was Robert's reproach making itself felt by a quicker, fiercer, more overpowering love, which had awakened within her toward him. Above all, there was understanding. She felt as if a mist had been lifted from her eyes, enabling her to look upon and comprehend the significance of life, that monster made up of beauty and brutality. But among the conflicting sensations which assailed her, there was neither shame nor remorse. There was a dull pang of regret because it was not the kiss of love which had inflamed her, because it was not love which had held this cup of life to her lips.

Thus Edna begins to understand herself as one who possesses "life, that monster made up of beauty and brutality." Although contradictory emotions boil within her, she accepts them with tremendous honesty, refusing to feel "shame" or "remorse," yet recognizing her own "brutality" in reaching out for the "beauty" of sexual fulfillment.

Edna's Hopeless Plight

Nothing in the novel makes the hopelessness of Edna's demand to be recognized as an autonomous individual more tragically apparent than does Alcée Arobin's behavior after he seduces her. Immediately he assumes a proprietary air as authoritative as Léonce's. Coming to her home, "he had found the front door open, and had followed his ring by walking in unceremoniously." When she moves out of Léonce's house, Arobin locks the door behind her and takes custody of the key. He comes uninvited to her house, where he reads the newspaper and smokes cigars as though he owns the entire establishment. One evening when she feels depressed and miserable, she demands that he leave. But "He did not answer, except to continue to caress her. He did not say good night until she had become supple to his gentle, seductive entreaties." Even Alcée Arobin, who "was absolutely nothing to her," believes that he owns Edna.

In her maternal role, as well, Edna encounters resistance to her desire to become a fully developed human individual. The same culture that deems woman to belong to man also demands her subordination to his offspring; Edna's society, therefore, abounds with "mother-women," who "idolized their children, worshiped their husbands, and esteemed it a holy privilege to efface themselves as individuals."

Since Edna is not one of these, her husband believes that she fails somehow as a mother. During their first quarrel, described above, he reproaches her "habitual neglect of the children." A little later, the narrator comments: "It would have been a difficult matter for Mr. Pontellier to define to his own satisfaction or any one else's wherein his wife failed in her duty toward their children. It was something which he felt rather than perceived." His feeling clearly does not derive from evidence of neglect in the boys' behavior, because they are remarkably self-sufficient, well-adjusted children:

> If one of the little Pontellier boys took a tumble whilst at play, he was not apt to rush to his mother's arms for comfort; he would more likely pick himself up, wipe the water out of his eyes and the sand out of his mouth, and go on

playing. Tots as they were, they pulled together and stood their ground in childish battles with doubled fists and up-lifted voices, which usually prevailed against the other mother-tots. . . .

In short, Mrs. Pontellier was not a mother-woman. The mother-women seemed to prevail that summer at Grand Isle.

Thus Chopin carefully, though subtly, establishes that Edna does not neglect her children. She neglects only her mother-woman image.

Edna tries on one occasion to explain to Adéle how she feels about her children and about herself. She says: "I would give up the unessential; I would give my money, I would give my life for my children; but I wouldn't give myself. I can't make it more clear; it's only something which I am beginning to comprehend, which is revealing itself to me." The "some-thing . . . which is revealing itself" does not become com-pletely clear to Edna herself until just before the end, when she does indeed give her life but not her self for her children's sake.

Edna expresses greater warmth toward her children when she feels happy and confident. Thus she treats the little boys with special tenderness after spending a happy day with Rob-ert on a nearby island; but after Robert goes to Mexico, "Edna tapped her foot impatiently, and wondered why the children persisted in playing in the sun when they might be under the trees. She went down and led them out of the sun, scolding the quadroon for not being more attentive." The morning af-ter she has tried to crush her wedding ring with her boot heel, Edna regards the children as "part and parcel of an alien world which had suddenly become antagonist." But when she learns that Robert is returning from Mexico, she sends "a huge box of bonbons" to the children, along with a "tender mes-sage" and "an abundance of kisses."

A few days after moving into her own small house—when "she began to look with her own eyes; to see and to apprehend the deeper undercurrents of life"—she goes to Iberville and spends a beautiful week with the boys, who are completely happy there on the plantation in the possessive care of Léonce's mother. Plainly, they do not need their mother, but they are glad to see her. And,

> How glad she was to see the children! She wept for very pleasure when she felt their little arms clasping her. . . . And what stories they had to tell their mother! About the pigs, the cows, the mules! . . . It was a thousand times more fun to haul real chips for old lame Susie's real fire than to drag painted blocks along the banquette on Esplanade Street! . . .
>
> . . . She lived with them a whole week long, giving them all of herself, and gathering and filling herself with their young existence.

Edna clearly loves her children, but she does not confuse her own life with theirs. When she leaves them, "She carried away with her the sound of their voices and the touch of their cheeks. . . . But by the time she had regained the city the song no longer echoed in her soul. She was again alone."

A Full Human Existence Is Inaccessible

When Edna leaves Adèle after the painful childbirth "scene of torture," which Edna has witnessed "with a flaming, outspoken revolt against the ways of Nature," Adèle gasps, "Think of the children, Edna. Oh think of the children." And Edna does "think of the children." She tells Dr. Mandelet vaguely: "I want to be let alone. Nobody has any right—except children, perhaps—and even then, it seems to me—or it did seem—." She returns home and, after discovering that even Robert does not recognize her right to autonomy, she lies awake all night thinking. She knows now who she is:

> She had said over and over to herself: "To-day it is Arobin; to-morrow it will be some one else. . . . it doesn't matter

about Léonce Pontellier—but Raoul and Etienne!" She understood now clearly what she had meant long ago when she said to Adèle Ratignolle that she would give up the unessential, but she would never sacrifice herself for her children.

... The children appeared before her like antagonists who had overcome her; who had overpowered and sought to drag her into the soul's slavery for the rest of her days. But she knew a way to elude them.

Thus woman's existence, first and last, intertwines with her maternal nature. Edna's sense of herself as a complete person makes impossible her role of wife and mother as defined by her society; yet she discovers that her role of mother also makes impossible her continuing development as an autonomous individual. So her thoughts as she walks into the sea comment profoundly on the special identity problems Chopin believes that women face: "She thought of Léonce and the children. They were a part of her life. But they need not have thought that they could possess her, body and soul." Unable to have a full human existence, Edna chooses to have none at all.

Contemporary
Perspectives on
Women's Issues

Sexism Is Flourishing in America

Barbara J. Berg

Barbara J. Berg is an American historian and feminist who has taught at Sarah Lawrence College, Yale Medical School, Columbia University, the Academy of Medicine, and Horace Mann School. She has written for a variety of publications, including the New York Times Magazine, *the* Washington Post, Ms., *and* Working Woman.

The rights won by the feminists of the twentieth century are being eroded in the new millennium, claims Barbara J. Berg in the following viewpoint. From an era of having too many choices, women now have too few, as they are forced into positions where decisions are made for them. Sexism is alive in politics, work, and education, and it is spread by a popular culture that reinforces the image of women as sexual objects or mommies, argues Berg. The reasons for this inequality are complex, but some possible causes can be found in the fears caused by terrorist attacks, the macho environment created by continuing wars in Iraq and Afghanistan, and the influence of right-wing media.

"Alive and well?" my dentist asks. "After Hillary [Clinton] almost got the Democratic nomination, and Sarah Palin had the number-two spot on the Republican ticket, how can you say sexism is alive and well?" I wonder if he'd say Barack Obama's presidency has obliterated racial discrimination in America, but before I can ask, he says, "Besides, with so much wrong in this country, why are you worrying about women?"

He lifts a dental mirror and curette from the tray. Since I have a policy never to argue with someone about to put sharp

Barbara J. Berg, "Introduction: Inequality: The New Normal," *Sexism in America: Alive, Well, and Ruining Our Future*. Chicago: Chicago Review Press, 2009, pp. ix–xix. Copyright © 2009 by the Chicago Review Press. Reproduced by permission.

instruments in my mouth, I don't respond as I want to. But my dentist, thoughtful and progressive though he is, has just proven my point. Women are *part* of this country—51 percent of it. And the problems facing us as a nation fall mightily upon them.

Recent Elections Prove Sexism Is Rampant

Hillary Clinton's candidacy did show women's potential even as it encouraged the Republicans' misguided attempt to woo her supporters with the VP [vice presidential] nomination of Sarah Palin. Yet neither candidate, although worlds apart in experience, knowledge, and commitment to women's rights, managed to escape the cage of gender politics—a cage fortified by retrograde media coverage.

Senator Clinton, presenting herself as the most qualified presidential contender, who just happened to have an X chromosome, encountered fierce resistance from a press determined to peg her as a "feminazi." And when the strategy of selecting Governor Palin—intended to buoy up a faltering [John] McCain campaign—sank beneath the weight of its own cynical miscalculations, Palin too became drenched in a tsunami of criticism with a distinctly antifemale hue. "Arm candy," "ditz," "shopaholic," "diva"—charges torpedoed from in- and outside the Beltway [the freeway encircling Washington, DC]. With incredible speed, Palin descended from it girl to mean girl to—in the wake of Team McCain's mudslinging fest—gossip girl.

However much the 2008 election ushered in the stunning historic breach of the racial divide, it also dredged up—and reinforced—chronically familiar ways of demeaning women. The issue of sexism in America, a nonstarter for decades, suddenly flashed before our eyes. A hot topic one week, it cooled considerably the next. But the animosity revealed during the campaigns was only a small outcropping from the solid bedrock of misogyny.

Hillary Clinton appears in Des Moines, Iowa, on January 27, 2007, as part of her campaign for the 2008 presidential election. Mandel Ngan/AFP/Getty Images.

A new and particularly virulent form of sexism is taking root throughout the country. . . .

Popular Culture Objectifies Women

"For God's sake! Why don't they leave her alone?" my friend Roz blurted out. We had just joined a few young women who'd gathered around the television in my son Andrew's apartment to watch [TV news anchor] Katie Couric on CBS while waiting for the other guests to arrive.

It was October 31, Andrew's birthday. Ever since he was a baby we've thrown him Halloween-themed birthday parties. Over the years they've become an honored tradition, even though Andrew is out of college and now hosts the parties himself. We no longer bob for apples or go trick-or-treating, but we still dress up in costumes, munch from bowls of candy corn, and use my husband Arnie's intricately carved pumpkins for decoration. Best of all, Andrew's Halloween birthday parties remain a gathering of relatives, longtime family friends, classmates, and colleagues—ours as well as our children's. In short, an eclectic mix of backgrounds and ages, somehow always managing to work.

"I liked Katie's 'Hi everyone' and eager smile," Roz continued. "She was really refreshing. Now she's all manned up."

"But that's what they wanted," Lisa, one of Andrew's friends, put in. "There were so many negative vibes about her girlishness. Didn't someone, Dan Rather, I think, accuse the network of going 'tarty' with her?"

"I hate it when men say things like that," my niece, Nancy, said. "Most of the female associates at my firm wear the dark-suit uniform, but there's one who's a little less conservative. She's not over the top by any means, but the guys call her the Law Whore."

"Speaking of whore," my daughter Alison said, quickly glancing at the others' outfits—either homemade or of the traditional black cat or witch variety—"wasn't this year's selection of costumes awful? That's why I decided to go as a Mets fan. It was either this"—she pointed to her team jersey—"or Miss Sexy Sergeant, the Promiscuous Pirate, or some version of it. Everything in the stores looked like leftovers from a *Playboy* photo shoot. I don't ever remember it being like this."

"If you think it's bad for us, it's even worse for little girls," Danielle, another friend, said. "I couldn't find anything in the stores for Hannah that didn't make her look like a six-year-old slut. And it's not just the costumes; it's toys, dolls—everything. Even though I swore I'd never allow it, Hannah is now the proud 'mother' of two Bratz dolls."

Danielle glanced around. "What? You don't know about Bratz?" A few of us didn't. "They're so seductive they could be strippers. Compared to them, Barbie looks like your wholesome next-door neighbor. Hannah's friends don't even play with Barbie anymore—too babyish! They all have Bratz. I was one of the holdout moms, but Hannah got a Yasmin Bratz and a Baby Bratz for her birthday—it made me nuts. And the mothers who gave them to her are really great, they're intelligent. Why aren't they bothered that their daughters are playing with dolls that look like pole dancers?"

"Well, pole dancing is very new wave," Lisa said. I didn't really know her and couldn't tell if she was trying to be funny. "It's just the way our culture is. Look at TV," she continued. "Maybe I shouldn't admit this, but I'm absolutely addicted to *Beauty and the Geek*. One part of me is comparing myself to the contestants. Am I as thin? How did Andrea get her hair that way? But another part hates it when the girls say they use their looks to get what they want. And they're encouraged to act like such idiots. The other night when Drew, who's a major geek, talked about Excel, the girls giggled and mouthed, 'What's that?' The show pushes the same old stereotypes about women. We can't be both smart and pretty, so, of course, it's better to be a bimbo than brainy if we want to be happy."

Redefining Happiness

"I guess that's why so many of my friends are getting boob jobs and tummy tucks," our daughter Laura, from Arnie's first marriage, chimed in. "You remember Vickie?" I nodded. "Well, she had everything fixed. And I mean *everything*."

"She did?" Ali and I gasped in unison. Vickie was Laura's friend from middle school. "I always thought she looked fine," I said. Laura agreed. "But I think she was feeling like, with the kids' schedules driving her nuts and Mark working all the time, she wanted to do something for herself."

For a minute or so no one said anything. Then a woman named Stephanie, a friend of my niece's, spoke. "I can totally relate to your friend," she said to Laura in a voice barely rising above a whisper. "I can't remember the last time I did anything just for myself. Don't get me wrong; I love my kids, and it was my decision to stop work. But Jack outearned me by a lot, there was no decent child care available, and I wasn't in love with the different nannies we had. When we were in the city, we managed, but when we moved to Connecticut the thought of commuting to my office and juggling the boys' schedules and all the after-school stuff was overwhelming."

She paused and glanced around, I think to make sure her husband was out of earshot, then started speaking again in a voice full of emotion. "Once I stayed home, Jack started doing less and less. He doesn't have a clue how insane my days are, how I never have a moment to myself. When I try to point this out to him, it's like I'm background noise; he's not paying any attention. Sometimes when I'm going to pick up one of the kids at karate or something, and I hear a song on the radio that reminds me of when I was younger, I just start to cry. This is so not what I expected."

"Amen to that," said one of Andrew's neighbors, a woman in her thirties. "When I landed my job at Morgan Stanley I couldn't believe how lucky I was. Now I'm not so sure. I started the same year as a few guys in my Dartmouth graduating class. And believe me, I'm already seeing the difference between their careers and mine. Two have been promoted to managing director, and their compensations are off the charts. And the thing is, I just got married; I don't even have kids yet. And already I'm hearing comments from these guys like 'When are we going to see a baby bump?' All of a sudden, I'm not taken as seriously. I feel that women get penalized just for having a working womb. I never say anything about it because I don't want them to think I'm not a team player. I keep thinking I should have gone into another field, but my friends at different jobs are having the same experiences. At least I know I'm on the cutting edge," she said with a forced laugh.

Today's Women Feel Powerless

I listened to these women with an accumulating sense of sadness. What accounted for the undercurrent of malaise so evident in their stories? Evident even though they tried to lighten the dark edges with humor. Evident even though they were all economically comfortable, freed from worries about affordable housing and child care. Here were these women—all beneficiaries of decades of feminism and assumed to enjoy unlimited possibilities for fulfillment and happiness—sounding like members of a 1970s consciousness-raising group. The terminology was different. Words like *objectified* or *second-class citizen* never made their way into the night's conversation as they surely would have back then. But the vulnerability, the sense of powerlessness, and the deep awareness of being treated and even *feeling* that you were somehow a lesser person—that was all there. And it troubled me.

I couldn't stop thinking about it. Not for days, even weeks, after. Why were these women, with so much going for them, slipping into roles rather than deciding upon them? Were these women a skewed sample? Or were they representative of the general population? . . .

Still a Man's World

What's the truth about women's lives in the new millennium?

I called on experts in a variety of fields, groups of former students, colleagues, young mothers, friends, women I'd interviewed years back for a book I wrote on balancing work and motherhood—women of different ages, backgrounds, experiences, and starting points.

Here's a small sample of what I heard:

When Alexi, a lawyer in New Jersey who'd given birth to twins, returned to work after her maternity leave was up, she thought she was doing the right thing. Instead, the partners said, "I can't believe you're back so soon" and "How could you leave your babies so young?"

"They made me feel as though I was doing something unnatural by coming back to work. It was awful," Alexi told me. "And I became aware of a difference in the way I was being treated. Then I looked around and saw something I'd never noticed before: all the partners are men, except one, and she's not married."

On a different front, thirty-year-old Julia told me, "I still can't believe this happened at one of the biggest hospitals in Chicago. Even though my obstetrician told me that the fetus wasn't growing, the heartbeat was slow, and we were headed for serious trouble, he refused to do an abortion." Not one doctor in the entire practice—eight in all—would do it. Their answer, according to Julia, was "Wait until you miscarry naturally." But the doomed pregnancy took its toll on Julia, her husband, and their three-year-old daughter. With Planned Parenthood booked for six weeks, as a last resort Julia ended up at a dirty, overcrowded abortion clinic, "a horrible, horrible experience," she said.

And on yet another, Evelyn, a home-health aide who couldn't afford private hospital care, described how doctors in an emergency room casually dismissed her seven-year-old daughter's coughing and labored breathing as a "bad cold." Evelyn urged further testing, but they simply sent the pair home. Three days later, when her daughter's temperature spiked to 106 followed by a convulsion, the ER doctors finally ordered a chest X-ray and discovered the pneumonia Evelyn had worried about from the start.

I spoke to thirteen- and fourteen-year-old girls at the best private schools who had to give the boys blow jobs before they were allowed to join lunchtime sports events, incidents of sexual harassment at a top California law school left unaddressed because the female students were afraid to jeopardize their positions, cadets at our service academies so casually viewing pornography online that they didn't even attempt to hide it when faculty walked over.

A health care expert told me about cuts in the budget of the FDA [Food and Drug Administration] Office of Women's

Health that were so extreme they threatened to halt all the office's activities and programs for the rest of the fiscal year. An executive recruiter enumerated the loss of female-held jobs in math, computer science, and engineering as well as in the Fortune 500 companies. The head of a public relations firm confided her concern about the lack of positive role models for girls, leading them to "emulate the antics of the Brit Pack, whose lives seem to be so much more powerful than their own." A college professor friend detailed what the rollbacks in Title IX will mean to her students. A journalist noted how many female bylines are disappearing from our mainstream press.

Inequality and Harassment in All Corners

I learned about Angie, by all accounts a competent and doting young mother, whose ex-husband and new wife were awarded custody of her three-year-old son because Angie was temporarily out of work. I spoke to Jeannie, who left her MBA [master of business administration] program because her boyfriend wanted her to become a teacher. There was Jessica, brutally raped in the ladies' room of a New York club and nearly talked out of bringing charges against her assailant by a demeaning and harassing law enforcement team. And Kathy, who would have continued working on Wall Street if she'd had daughters so she'd be a strong role model to them, but with two sons, didn't think it mattered.

And then this, from a former student in my women's history course who has remained close to my family:

Two months ago I went to speak to one of the partners about a brief I'd written. We were just getting started when he said, "You know, Emily, with legs like yours, you don't have to worry about writing a decent brief." I said, "I'm going to pretend I didn't hear that," and he continued like nothing had happened.

But whenever the partner saw Emily after that, he'd make some little sexual remark. "It made me really uncomfortable," she said. "I mean, this kind of thing isn't acceptable in the workplace anymore. Right?"

Emily approached the executive director of the firm, who advised her, "Don't take everything so seriously. The guy's only kidding with you. If you want to stay here you better get used to it. It's a man's world."

"End of story," Emily said, her voice drooping with resignation. "Now I keep hoping I didn't hurt my career."

I simply shook my head, too stunned to say anything. But I couldn't escape feeling that I'd let her down.

In Denial of Increasing Sexism

Listening closely, I detected a definable thread running through these women's stories—a bending, an acquiescence to situations and conditions seemed shaped to accommodate needs and interests at variance with their own. I became aware of a palpable lack of agency, of validation, a lack of real control over everyday existence reaching across boundaries of geography, class, race, and age. It was as if we were being marginalized in our own stories. What [French philosopher] Simone de Beauvoir, writing in an earlier era, famously called the experience of being "the other."

I knew it was becoming commonplace to think of American women, particularly those of the middle class, as suffering from a "too muchness," a glut of options and choices. But I began to question that interpretation. "Choice" is a knotty concept, and, excepting its relevance to reproductive rights, it doesn't necessarily equate with freedom and empowerment. True, we can now "choose" to drive ourselves nuts over getting our children into the best preschools, to go under the plastic surgeon's knife three times a year, to keep working for a boss who refuses to grant well-deserved promotions, to take our chances without health insurance, to get up on a bar and dance topless. But we should all be encouraged to take a hard look at the conditions influencing these choices, to examine what pressures women feel and what limitations are imposed by intractable social and economic institutions, unfriendly business communities, and unresponsive government.

Far from hearing about a "too muchness" in women's lives, I perceived, in fact, a sense of *too little*. Women confessed to feelings of loss, to a generalized insecurity about their futures, to something very wrong at the core of their existence. These emotions weren't expressed as complaints or grievances. Most women accepted the difficulties they encountered. They saw them as individual issues, even as their own fault—as life. . . .

I discovered renewed sexism in our national policies and our jobs; on college campuses, the Internet, and major television shows; and in our most intimate relations—an unequivocal resurgence of sexism in this country so potent, so complexly and broadly expressed, so much a product of the twenty-first century, it should be called nothing less than the sexism of mass destruction. Yet astonishingly, the nation is in a collective state of denial over this deepening misogyny and these growing gender inequities. It's as if we'd rather believe that the emperor really has new clothes than confront the naked truth.

A dangerous and startling trend is short-circuiting the inheritance of feminism in every aspect of women's lives. Roles are being redefined both *for* us and *with* us. Measured by every standard, women's independence and self-determination are being eroded. The world of equal rights and treatment that so many of us struggled for, the one I believed and hoped we were still working to achieve, is slowly but most definitely coming apart.

I'm not talking about a repressive Republic of Gilead [an imaginary totalitarian country that is the setting For Margaret Atwood's *The Handmaid's Tale*] somewhere in our future, but a danger at our very doorsteps.

Many Factors Led to This Point

How have we gotten to this point? What has become of the movement dedicated to winning respect for all women—the most significant social revolution of the twentieth century? When did we start to lose our voice? Our sense of authenticity? Our autonomy?

When did inequality start to feel normal again?

Being trained as a historian, I tend to seek understanding in the past. My mind started pedaling back through all the terrible and traumatic experiences our nation has weathered—times of vast uncertainty, sharp pain, and collective grief, when the moorings upon which we'd anchored our lives seemed to be slipping from under us and made us rethink and sometimes reconfigure deeply held notions of gender, sexuality, fairness, sacrifice, responsibility. Without a doubt, we are living through one such time.

I wondered, How much have our anxieties in the wake of [the terrorist attacks of] 9/11 and in the face of the continuing threat of terrorism made us yearn for the security of traditional roles? To what extent have the war in Iraq and the subsequent masculinization of American politics and culture affected women's position in society? In what ways have the devastating pincers of financial uncertainty narrowed opportunities to escape gender stereotypes?

I thought about how thirty years of conservative influence—the millionaire-backed, prominently placed right-wing think tanks and their media machines—might have impacted our policies and ideas. How the climate of absolutes—good versus evil, us versus them—and the either/or mentality of our nation have shaped our perceptions about gender roles and how we lead our lives, making us believe there's only *one* way to be a good mother, wife, human being. I wondered whether we've become distracted from the real issues uniting women by the media-manipulated "cat fights." Whether we've become so immersed in the ethos of individualism that we've forgotten one another, and so obsessed with celebrity culture we've lost sight of ourselves.

As I looked back over my list of questions, I realized there'd be no simple explanation, no one cause, but an array of multifaceted and overlapping factors, what one of my dissertation advisers, the late [American historian and social critic] Arthur Schlesinger Jr., called "the chronic obscurity of events."

Focus, Not Balance, Is the Secret to Women's Happiness

Marcus Buckingham

Marcus Buckingham is an author, researcher, and consultant. He is the founder of TMBC, a management consulting firm, and his books include The Truth About You.

Many of today's successful women are overcommitted and stressed out by lives that place too many demands on them, Marcus Buckingham contends in the following viewpoint. Their problem is, he argues, that they mistake "having it all" with doing it all. Happiness comes when women focus on what's important to them and cut out superfluous activities, Buckingham maintains.

Recently, my wife, Jane, attended a forum in California organized by the governor's wife, Maria Shriver. The Women's Conference, as it was called, brought together thousands of the most influential and accomplished women in the world, among them feminist icon Gloria Steinem. After her talk, a woman asked Ms. Steinem if she could explain what she meant by "You can have it all" when, the woman continued, "We clearly can't have it all."

Women Pay a Price for "Having It All"

The gist of Ms. Steinem's reply was that she'd been misunderstood. She never said, "You can have it all." What she said was that she didn't think men, or society at large, should define women's choices. Women should be able to make any choice they wanted. But, according to Gloria Steinem herself, she never said, "You can have it all."

Marcus Buckingham, "Introduction: The Opposite of Juggling," *Find Your Strongest Life: What the Happiest and Most Successful Women Do Differently*. Toronto: Thomson Nelson, 2009. Copyright © 2009 by Thomson Nelson Book Group. Reproduced by permission of The Marcus Buckingham Company (TMBC).

Jane told me this story over dinner that night. Jane is a re-markable woman. She wrote her first book at sixteen, and par-layed that success into a multimillion-dollar company with of-fices in New York and Los Angeles. She's an author and television presenter, a fantastic mother, and everything I could ever want in a wife. But she's also someone who will freely ad-mit that she may have pushed too hard in trying to have it all. She is the kind of mother who is determined to pick up our children, Jack and Lilia, from school every afternoon even if it means juggling calls and keeping one eye on her BlackBerry. When she's invited to appear on *Good Morning America* or the *Today* show in New York, she'll insist on taking the red-eye from our home in Los Angeles so she won't miss Jack's pitch-ing or Lilia's ballet practice. And after the show, she'll take the earliest plane back to the office. As a woman who has built a happy and loving family while simultaneously thriving as an entrepreneur, Jane seems to have succeeded in living up to everyone's ideal.

Yet Jane knows full well that there is a price to be paid for trying to have it all. She knows how hard it is to let go of work when she's with the kids, and to let go of the kids when she's hard at work. She knows she sometimes runs on too little sleep. She has had migraines that withstood everything she hit them with. And she even, on a couple of scary occa-sions, has fainted during presentations.

So, the way I see it, on hearing Ms. Steinem's comment, "I never said women could have it all," Jane would have been en-tirely within her rights to throw up her hands in righteous frustration and say, "Thanks, Gloria. Thanks very much. Couldn't you have told us this twenty years ago? It would have made my life a heck of a lot easier."

But she didn't. Righteous frustration is not Jane's style. In-stead, she just looked at me across the dining table and smiled, "Does that mean my life's a typo?"

Many women struggle to balance their professional and parental roles. Marcus Buckingham argues that happiness is achieved not by trying to "have it all" but rather by identifying and focusing on what is most important to oneself. Poulsons Photography/ Shutterstock.com.

Focusing on What Is Important

Jane's joking aside, is Gloria Steinem right? Is it impossible for women to "have it all?" On the surface, it would seem so. Trying to be all things to all people all of the time is a fool's game that will, in the end, drain mind, body, and spirit.

But dig a little deeper and you have to ask yourself, "What's the alternative?" If Jane tells herself that she can't have it all, then what's she left with? Three-quarters of a life? Half a life? Less than half? An approach to life that begins with the question, "Which parts of myself must I cut out?" inevitably leads to a laundry list of unhealthy emotions: panic that you can't cut out enough, confusion over which parts to cut out, fear that you've cut out the wrong parts, guilt about that fear, and resentment about all of it.

Jane shouldn't be asking herself, "Which parts of myself should I cut out?" Nor should you. It's the wrong question.

The right question is, "What do I mean by 'having it all'?" Because if "having it all" means drawing enough strength from life to feel fulfilled, loved, successful, and in control, then that is something every single one of us should aim for and every single one of us can attain.

"Having it all" doesn't mean having everything, all at once, all the time. "Having it all" means taking yourself seriously. It means knowing yourself well enough to find your purpose in life. It means knowing what needs to change when you sense that you've lost that purpose. It means having the faith to believe that change is possible and having the courage to make those changes. It means drawing strength from the relationships in your life, and, if there's no strength to be drawn, knowing when to cut those relationships out of your life.

It means mastering the skill of using life to fill you up. That is all you can do, and it is everything you need to do.

The conventional image of a successful woman today is that she's a virtuoso juggler, somehow moving fast enough to keep all the many aspects of her busy life in the air at the same time. Conventional it may be, but it's also quite sad. The core skill of juggling is throwing, not catching. To keep every object in the air, you have to get rid of each one as quickly as possible, barely allowing it to register on your fingertips before you toss it up and away, preparing for the next object to throw.

A strong life is the opposite of juggling. Juggling requires you to keep everything at bay, up in the air, away from you. The secret to living a strong life lies in knowing how to draw a few things in toward you. It asks you to be discriminating, selective, intentional. You can find energizing moments in each aspect of your life, but to do so you must learn how to catch them, hold on to them, feel the pull of their weight, and allow yourself to follow where they lead.

Feminism Is Relevant to Today's Young Women

Jessica Valenti

Jessica Valenti is the founder and executive editor of the blog Feministing.com. She has written for AlterNet, Salon, and the British newspaper the Guardian.

Contrary to what you see in the media, feminism is not dead, states Jessica Valenti in the following viewpoint. Feminism has a bad rap today, with commentators arguing that feminists are anti-men, that feminists have achieved their goal, or that feminists are responsible for a variety of evils from the demise of the family unit to persecution of Michael Jackson. The reality is, Valenti contends, that feminism is a positive movement, dedicated to making things better for all humanity, and it is alive and well.

What's the worst possible thing you can call a woman? Don't hold back, now.

You're probably thinking of words like slut, whore, bitch, cunt (I told you not to hold back!), skank.

Okay, now, what are the worst things you can call a guy? Fag, girl, bitch, pussy. I've even heard the term "mangina."

Notice anything? The worst thing you can call a girl is a girl. The worst thing you can call a guy is a girl. Being a woman is the ultimate insult. Now tell me that's not royally f---ed up. Recognizing the screwed nature of this little exercise doesn't necessarily make you a feminist. But it should. Most young women know that something is off. And even if we know that some things are sexist, we're certainly not ready to say we're feminists. It's high time we get past the "I'm not a feminist, but . . ." stuff. You know what I'm talking about: "I'm not a feminist or anything, but it is total bullshit that Wal-Mart won't fill my birth control prescription."

Do you think it's fair that a guy will make more money doing the same job as you? Does it piss you off and scare you when you find out about your friends getting raped? Do you ever feel like shit about your body? Do you ever feel like something is wrong with you because you don't fit into this bizarre ideal of what girls are supposed to be like?

Well, my friend, I hate to break it to you, but you're a hardcore feminist. I swear.

Feel-Good Feminism

For some reason, feminism is seen as super anti: anti-men, anti-sex, anti-sexism, anti-everything. And while some of those antis aren't bad things, it's not exactly exciting to get involved in something that's seen as so consistently negative.

The good news is, feminism isn't all about antis. It's progressive and—as cheesy as this sounds—it's about making your life better. As different as we all are, there's one thing most young women have in common: We're all brought up to feel like there's something wrong with us. We're too fat. We're dumb. We're too smart. We're not ladylike enough—*stop cursing, chewing with your mouth open, speaking your mind.* We're too slutty. We're not slutty enough.

F--- that.

You're not too fat. You're not too loud. You're not too smart. You're not unladylike. *There is nothing wrong with you.*

I know it sounds simple, but it took me a hell of a long time to understand this. And once I did, damn, did it feel good. Why go through your life believing you're not good enough and that you have to change?

Feminism not only allows you to see through the bullshit that would make you think there's something wrong with you, but also offers ways to make you feel good about yourself and to have self-respect without utilizing any mom-popular sayings, like "Keep your legs together," or boy-popular screamings, like "Show me your tits!"

Really, imagine how nice it would be to realize that all the stuff you've been taught that makes you feel crappy just isn't true. It's like self-help times one hundred.

But all that said, I really do understand the hesitancy surrounding the f-word [feminism]. My own experience with the exercise that kicked off this chapter—"What's the worst possible thing you can call a woman?"—was presented by a professor on the first day of a women's literature class after she asked how many of us were feminists. Not one person raised a hand. Not even me. My excuse-ridden thinking was, *Oh, there's so many kinds of feminism, how can I say I know what they're all about? Blah, blah, blah. I'm a humanist blah, blah, blah.* Bullshit. When I think back on it, I knew I was a feminist. I was just too damn freaked out to be the only one raising her hand.

Most young women *are* feminists, but we're too afraid to say it—or even to recognize it. And why not? Feminists are supposed to be ugly. And fat. And hairy! Is it f----- up that people are so concerned about dumb, superficial stuff like this? Of course. Is there anything wrong with being ugly, fat, or hairy? Of course not. But let's be honest: No one wants to be associated with something that is seen as uncool and unattractive. But the thing is, feminists are pretty cool (and attractive!) women.

So let's just get all the bullshit stereotypes and excuses out of the way.

But Feminists Are Ugly!

Yawn. Honestly, this is the most tired stereotype ever. But it's supersmart in its own way. Think about it, ladies. What's the one thing that will undoubtedly make you feel like shit? Someone calling you ugly.

Back in fifth grade, the love of my life was Douglas Mac-Intyre, who told me I'd be pretty if only I didn't have such a big, ugly nose. I shit you not when I say that for months, every day after school I would stand in front of the three-way mirror in my bathroom, staring at the offending body part and trying to figure out how a nose could go so horribly, horribly wrong.

Ugly stays with you. It's powerful, and that's why the stereotype is so perfect. The easiest way to keep women—especially young women—away from feminism is to threaten them with the ugly stick. It's also the easiest way to dismiss someone and her opinions. ("Oh, don't listen to her—she's just pissed 'cause she's ugly.")

Seems stupid, right? I mean, really, what's with this *na-na-na-boo-boo* kind of argument? Have you ever heard of a Republican saying, "Oh, don't be a Democrat; they're all ugly"? Of course not, because that would be ridiculous. But for some reason, ridiculous is commonplace when it comes to the f-word.

For example, conservative radio host Rush Limbaugh says that feminism was established "to allow unattractive women easier access to the mainstream of society." Okay—have you ever *seen* Rush Limbaugh? Yeah, enough said. Oh, and by the way—I think I'm pretty hot now. So screw you, Douglas MacIntyre.

But Things Are Fine the Way They Are!

What do I know? Maybe things are fine for you. Maybe you're lucky and superprivileged and you wake up in the morning to birds chirping and breakfast in bed and all that good stuff. But chances are, that's not the case.

There are plenty of folks who argue that feminism has achieved its goal. The 1998 *Time* magazine article "Is Feminism Dead?" said, "If the women's movement were still useful, it would have something to say; it's dead because it has won."

There's no doubt that women have made progress, but just because we get to vote and have the "right" to work doesn't mean things are peachy keen. Anyone who thinks women have "won," that all is well and good now, should ask why the president of Harvard can say that maybe women are naturally worse at math and then have people actually take him seriously. Or why a teacher can still get fired for being pregnant and unmarried.

Seriously, are things really cool the way they are when so many of us are upchucking our meals and getting raped and beat up and being paid less money than men? And being denied birth control, and being told not to have sex but be sexy, and a hundred other things that make us feel shitty?

Methinks not. It can be better. It has to be.

Feminism Is for Old White Ladies

This one didn't come out of nowhere. The part of the feminist movement that has been most talked about it, most written about, and most paid attention to is the rich-whitey part. For example, back in the '60s and '70s, white middle-class feminists were fighting for the right to work outside the home, despite the fact that plenty of not-so-privileged women were already doing exactly that. Because they had to.

Even now, issues of race and class come up in feminism pretty often. But unlike in days of yore, now they're being addressed. Besides, feminism isn't just about the organizations you see at protests, or what you hear about in the news. Feminist actions—particularly the kind spearheaded by younger women—are as diverse as we are. You'll see what I mean when you get to the end of this chapter: Young women are working their asses off for causes they believe in. Which is why this next stereotype is so very annoying.

Feminism Is So Last Week

Every once in a while, there's some big article about feminism being dead—the most famous of which is the aforementioned *Time* piece. And if feminism isn't dead, it's equally often accused of being outdated. Or a failure. Or unnecessary.

But if feminism is dead, then why do people have to keep on trying to kill it? Whether it's in the media, politics, or conservative organizations, there's a big old trend of trying to convince the world that feminism is long gone.

The argument is either that women don't need feminism anymore, or that those crazy radical feminists don't speak for most women. Never mind that recent polls show that most women support feminist goals, like equal pay for equal work, ending violence against women, childcare, women's healthcare, and getting more women in political office. Here comes that "I'm not a feminist, but . . ." stuff again!

The obsession with feminism's demise is laughable. And if the powers that be can't convince you that it's dead, that's when the blame game starts. Feminism is the media's favorite punching bag.

The horrors that feminism is supposedly responsible for range from silly contradictions to plainly ludicrous examples. In recent articles, feminism has been blamed for promoting promiscuity; promoting man-hating; the torture at Abu Ghraib [a prison in Iraq]; ruining "the family"; the feminization of men; the "failures" of Amnesty International; and even unfairness to Michael Jackson. I'm not kidding. You name it, feminism is the cause.

My all-time favorite accusation: Feminism is responsible for an increase in the number of women criminals. You're going to love this. Wendy Wright of Concerned Women for America—a conservative anti-feminist organization—is quoted in a 2005 article, "Rising Crime Among Women Linked to Feminist Agenda," as saying it's pesky feminists who are to blame for the increase of women in prison.

Wright claims that women are committing crimes because feminism has taught them that "women should not be dependent on others" and that "they don't need to be dependent on a husband," which inevitably forces them to "fend for themselves."

Got that, girls? Without a husband to depend on, you'll be selling crack in no time!

For something that is so tired and outdated, feminism certainly seems to be doing a lot of damage, huh?

Obviously there's an awful lot of effort being put into discrediting the f-word—but why all the fuss? If folks didn't see feminism as a threat—and a powerful one—they wouldn't spend so much time putting it down, which is part of what attracted me to feminism in the first place. I wanted to know what all the brouhaha was about.

It's important to remember that all of these stereotypes and scare tactics serve a specific purpose. If you think feminism is all about big fat ugly dykes, or is dead or racist, then you'll stay far the hell away from it.

'Cause don't forget—there are a lot of people benefiting from your feeling like shit about yourself. Think about it: If you don't feel fat, you won't buy firming lotions and diet pills and the like. If you don't feel stupid, you might speak out against all the screwy laws that adversely affect women. It pays—literally—to keep women half there. And god forbid you get involved in anything that would make you wonder why in the world women are having surgery to make their vaginas "prettier." (Sorry, I couldn't help but mention it; it's too freaky not to.)

The solution? Don't fall for it. If feminism isn't for you, fine. But find that out for yourself. I'm betting that you're more likely to be into something that encourages you to recognize that you're already pretty badass than something that insists you're a fat, dumb chick.

Defining Feminism

There are so many stereotypes about feminism, and so many different definitions of it, that what feminism actually is gets insanely confusing—even for women who have been working on women's issues for years. But I always was a fan of the dictionary definition. And I promise this is the only time I'll be quoting the frigging dictionary:

fem-i-nism

1. Belief in the social, political, and economic equality of the sexes.

2. The movement organized around this belief.

Hmm . . . don't see anything about man-hating in there. Or hairy legs. Obviously, there are tons of different kinds of feminism and schools of thought, but I'd say the above is enough to get you started. Besides, at the end of the day, feminism is really something you define for yourself.

Confusion over Feminism

No matter how clear-cut (or how complex) feminism can be, not all women are feminists by virtue of having ovaries. And that's just fine by me. I realized this in a big way recently. I was quoted in Rebecca Traister's 2005 *Salon.com* article entitled "The F-Word," airing my feelings about the word "feminist"—and I got a little pissy. "Part of me gets so angry at younger women who are nervous about feminism because they're afraid that boys won't like them. . . . Part of me wants to say, 'Yeah, someone's going to call you a lesbian. Someone's going to say you're a fat, ugly dyke. Suck it up.'" My attempt to strongly defend the word "feminism" didn't go over well with a lot of people. One woman actually posted a homophobic rant of a response to *Salon.com*:

> I'll call myself a feminist when the fat, mannish dykes who do run around calling themselves "Feminist" very loudly and

constantly concede that my decision to groom and dress myself as a twenty-first-century professional woman is every bit as valid a choice as their decision to become stereotypical jailhouse bulldaggers. Ovaries only make you female, they do not make you woman, and I am a woman. In other words, I will call myself a feminist when those mannabees are as proud of and joyful in their womanhood as I am in mine . . . Until then, f--- off and take your hairy legs with you.

Crazy, right? I didn't need much more than this to realize that feminism isn't for everybody. I never really bought the "We're all sisters" thing anyway. I've met enough racist, classist, homophobic women to know better. Feminism's power isn't in how many women identify with the cause. I'll take quality over quantity any day.

Quality Women Are Feminists

So who are these elusive feminists? Like I've said—you are, even if you don't know it yet. Though I'm hoping by now you're at least slightly convinced. The smartest, coolest women I know are feminists. And they're everywhere. You don't need to be burning bras (actually, this never happened—total myth) or standing on a picket line to be a feminist. Chances are, you've already done stuff that makes you a feminist. You don't have to be a full-time activist to be an awesome feminist.

The work that young women are doing across the country is pretty goddamn impressive. Do they all consider themselves feminists? Probably not. But a lot of the work they're doing is grounded in feminist values. Just a few examples:

A group of high school girls in Allegheny County, Pennsylvania, organized a "girlcott" of Abercrombie & Fitch [A&F] when the clothing company came out with a girls' shirt that read: *Who needs brains when you have these?* After the group caused quite a ruckus in the media, A&F pulled the shirt.

Two young women in Brooklyn, Consuelo Ruybal and Oraia Reid, used their own money to start an organization called RightRides after a number of young women were raped in their neighborhood. Women can call the service anytime from midnight to 4 AM on the weekends and get a free ride home. Simple, but damn effective. Their motto is: "Because getting home safe should not be a luxury."

The documentary film *The Education of Shelby Knox* was inspired by a high school student in Lubbock, Texas, who took on her town's school board to fight for comprehensive sex education. Shockingly, the abstinence-only brand they were receiving wasn't quite cutting it.

A group of queer women, tired of seeing the art world bypass great women artists, started *riffRAG* magazine. The magazine features work that slips under the mainstream's radar.

Misty McElroy decided to start Rock 'n' Roll Camp for Girls as part of a class project at Portland State University. She expected about twenty girls to sign up—she ended up getting three hundred. Rock 'n' Roll Camp for Girls teaches young girls to play instruments, deejay, sing, and write songs and ends with a live performance. The camp was so popular in Oregon that there are now rock camps in New York City; Washington, D.C.; Nashville, Tennessee; Tucson, Arizona; and various California locations.

This is just a small sampling of the amazing work young women are already doing (and they say we're apathetic!), and it doesn't even touch on all the women's blogs, online and print zines, and community programs that are out there. These women and their work prove that feminism is not only alive and well, but also energized and diverse. Not to mention fun.

You can be a feminist without making it your life's work. It's about finding the cause that works for you, and makes you happy, and doing something about it. (Trust me, getting off your ass can be more fun than you think.) For some women, that means working in women's organizations, fighting against sexist laws. For others, it means volunteering time to teach young girls how to deejay. It doesn't matter what you're doing, so long as you're doing something. Even if it's as simple as speaking up when someone tells a nasty-ass sexist joke.

There's a popular feminist shirt these days that reads: *This is what a feminist looks like.* Ashley Judd wore one at the 2004 pro-choice March for Women's Lives in Washington, D.C. Margaret Cho wore one on the Spring 2003 cover of *Ms.* magazine. I wear one, too; I love this shirt. Because you never really do know what a feminist looks like. And believe me, we're everywhere.

The Internet Helps Women Communicate

Kara Jesella

Kara Jesella is the coauthor of How "Sassy" Changed My Life: A Love Letter to the Greatest Teen Magazine of All Time. *She is a frequent culture contributor to the* New York Times, Salon, *the* American Prospect, *and other publications.*

The Internet has given mothers a new way to communicate with each other about the issues they face, claims Kara Jesella in the following viewpoint. Many "mommyblogs" deal with personal issues, but an increasing number address political concerns. And while the technology they are using today is new and different, the issues are the same—discrimination in the workplace, early childhood education, and publicly funded childcare, Jesella maintains.

"As a mother of three, there are very few things that are entirely mine," wrote Jill Smokler of Washington, D.C., in a recent post to her blog Scary Mommy.

Virtual Consciousness-Raising

"My bed is inevitably invaded by all of the kids sometime throughout the night. My favorite foods are devoured by mouths other than mine and my cosmetics are used for dress up these days as often as on my own face. My car is filled with car seats and stale Cheerios and my purse is so stuffed with junk for the kids that I can't even carry my own sunglass case. But this blog? It's mine. All mine. And that's what I love about it."

In the past, a mother feeling overwhelmed might have picked up the phone to call her best friend. Today, she also sits down at her computer and posts to her blog.

In the last few years, there has been a boom in "mommyblogs" such as Scary Mommy. Many of these chronicle the personal details of their writer's family lives, such as ex-Mormon stay-at-home-in-Salt-Lake-City mom Heather B. Armstrong's popular Dooce blog, which includes her sharing her struggle with postpartum depression. Mod Mom merges personal blogging with posts about design; Champuru does the same with food.

Not all the mommybloggers might self-define as feminists—although certainly there is a feminist impulse behind the avowed goal of many of them to change cultural perceptions of motherhood—but one might argue that what they're doing is a virtual version of feminist consciousness-raising: They're being exceedingly open about their experiences of mothering, and sharing those experiences in an (online) community with other mothers.

Mommyblogging Can Be Political

Though moms have been publicly admitting to their mixed feelings about motherhood for generations—for example, in 1976 [poet] Adrienne Rich compared herself to a monster in the feminist classic *Of Woman Born: Motherhood as Experience and Institution*—talking about trials and tribulations and publicly admitting to being "bad moms" is a political act in itself for many moms. Among mommybloggers, dark humor about bodily functions, blog names like "Her Bad Mother," and allusions to drinking martinis during naptime are de rigueur [required].

And in fact, a strong subset of the mommyblogosphere is overtly feminist and proudly activist. For example, Lawyer Mama, whose day job is as new media director for an organization that supports military families, posts pictures of herself with Nancy Pelosi [then Speaker of the House] and eulogized Dr. George Tiller [an assassinated abortionist]. Blogger Writes

Like She Talks names the 10 legislators hammering out the Ohio budget and notes ruefully that all are men.

Chicagoan Veronica Arreola notes that among women of color who blog, some are changing what counts as a motherhood issue to include working-class and lower-class issues, such as finding a full-time job, obtaining food stamps or changing immigration law. Arreola focuses her personal blog— Viva La Feminista—on feminism, motherhood and her Latina identity.

Many mommybloggers are concerned with subjects that immediately affect their family and children, such as universal health care and paid maternity leave. That's what got Lisa Frack of Portland, Ore., involved in political mommyblogging. In 2003, three months pregnant with her first child, she learned that her full-time federal job didn't provide paid maternity leave.

"What happens when my income disappears?" she wondered, since she earned a larger salary than her husband. Frack decided to educate herself, then asked a popular local mom blog if she could start writing for it about political issues that affect mothers. She soon founded a group of political moms called Activistas, and before long was collecting signatures at a farmer's market and corralling 20 busy moms on a Wednesday afternoon to join her at a state Senate hearing an hour away.

The Internet Makes It Easier to Organize

Overtly political mommybloggers are often affiliated with motherhood organizations that have developed a strong online presence, including Mothers & More, the Mothers Movement Online and the National Association of Mothers' Centers. Frack's group was inspired by MomsRising, an online organization (and blog site) that made the film *The Motherhood Manifesto* about the ways American society continues to discriminate against mothers—such as paying them less than men or women without children. These advocacy groups are often involved in trying to get pro-mom legislation passed and in encouraging direct action. Many affiliated mommy-bloggers publicize the groups' actions on their own blogs, encouraging other women to get involved.

In some places, the online movement has led to local legislative advocacy, with women lobbying, testifying on committees and making hundreds of phone calls to their legislators. Though the bill Frack worked on in Oregon didn't pass, there have been notable successes: With the help of motherhood activists, New Jersey passed the Family Leave Insurance bill, which . . . provides up to six weeks of benefits while a worker takes time off to bond with a new child or care for a family member with a serious health condition.

Since many of the political actions are coordinated online, it's easy for women, bloggers or not, to get active in the groups. Mothers & More, which has 7,500 members and over 100 chapters across the country, began as a personal support group and grew into an advocacy organization, says Joanne Brundage, the group's executive director.

"It's very different to be able to have direct access to people in their homes," adds Kristin Rowe-Finkbeiner, executive director of MomsRising—a group she cofounded with MoveOn.org's Joan Blades—which grew from 160,000 members to over a million in the last year [2008–2009]. She notes that women are busy, many are struggling economically, and they can't go to meetings for hours at a time. "That is huge to not have to leave home."

Old Issues, New Technology

The technology may be new, but the issues facing mothers aren't. In fact, the feminist movement has been working against pregnancy discrimination and for paid family leave, publicly funded child care and early childhood education for 40 years. Against great opposition, there have been some impressive successes, including the Pregnancy Discrimination Act of 1978, which makes it illegal for employers to treat pregnant workers differently than other employees, and the Family and Medical Leave Act of 1993, which provides eligible workers up to 12 weeks of unpaid time off to handle serious health conditions for themselves, care for a sick family member or care for a newborn or adopted child. There have also been setbacks, as in 1970 when President Richard Nixon vetoed a universal child-care bill, authored by Rep. Shirley Chisholm, claiming it would lead to the "Sovietization of American children."

Today, many mothers still find it grueling to juggle work and care for their families. A little more than half of employed U.S. women don't have one paid sick day for themselves or to care for family members, which means they lose money anytime they have to skip work because of an ill child. Pregnancy itself is the No. 1 cause of women's poverty. And seven out of 10 women—many of them moms—have no health insurance. . . .

Community Organizing Still Necessary

Many mothers may not start out intending to be political, but as they find their voices, their blogs evolve into forums for political commentary, says Joanne Bamberger, who blogs at Pundit Mom. "I think a lot of moms who don't identify as political activists or feminists are writing on sites increasingly about issues that are important to them." Then, as they get comfortable talking about their own mothering issues online, they are "finding their political selves."

But some longtime activists caution that the influx in online activism needs to be combined with a renewed commitment to on-the-ground grassroots organizing. "Getting paid leave passed is really hard work; you need to be working with people you can get to know and have solidarity with," says Judith Stadtman Tucker, founder of the Mothers Movement Online. Inspired by her work organizing for Barack Obama's presidential campaign, she is now spending less time blogging and more time doing face-to-face community organizing on motherhood issues in her home state of New Hampshire.

Other activists, meanwhile, think that the link between feminist blogs and mommyblogs needs to be strengthened. Says Arreola, "For me, right now, it's still about trying to connect motherhood and feminism. To get more feminist activists to jump on these mom issues and more moms to be politically active."

Adds Los Angeles mommyblogger JJ Keith on JJust Kidding, "We need young feminists, old feminists, non-feminists and everyone to see that our culture is making motherhood a private struggle that is being medicalized, commercialized . . . Americans have become accustomed to thinking of motherhood as a trial, but with some activism and support, it could be a joy again."

Suicide Is an Act of Asserting Control

Vanessa Grigoriadis

Vanessa Grigoriadis is a contributing editor at New York Magazine, Rolling Stone, *and* Vanity Fair.

The suicide of noted feminist and scholar Carolyn Heilbrun took many people, including her family, by surprise because she was in good mental and physical health, writes Vanessa Grigoriadis in the following viewpoint. In some ways, however, Heilbrun's suicide was entirely consistent with the way in which she chose to live her life. The freedom to choose was paramount to Heilbrun, Grigoriadis maintains, and getting to a point in life where her choices were limited would have been anathema to her.

Even if Carolyn Gold Heilbrun hadn't been a scholar of [writer] Virginia Woolf—"Carol created Bloomsbury [a group of intellectuals who met for informal discussions]," Anne Olivier Bell, Woolf's niece, once said—there would nevertheless be something about her suicide, on October 9 [2003], that would resonate with women's lives, much as Woolf's life did in [Michael Cunningham's novel] *The Hours*. Heilbrun is one of the mothers—perhaps the mother—of academic feminism, laying the groundwork for women's struggle over the past decades with what they called the "patriarchy."

A Moral Right to Suicide

Patriarchy was a word Heilbrun used often, and freely, even in 2003. She had strong opinions on things, particularly on women's issues, such as motherhood (not for everyone) and grandmotherhood (not for her); women's relationships with

Vanessa Grigoriadis, "A Death of One's Own," *New York Magazine*, December 8, 2003, pp. 40–46. Copyright © 2003 by New York Magazine. Reproduced by permission.

other women, which should be conciliatory to a fault; cooking Thanksgiving dinner, which in later years she would not. She took Woolf's concept of a room of one's own to heart. In fact, she had several. There was one at her sprawling Central Park West apartment, purchased for tens of thousands of dollars in the sixties, and another at her country house (she had a "bat house" nailed to that house's barn; Heilbrun loved bats). Then, when she was 68 years old, despite having three grown children, two grandchildren, and what by all accounts was a loving marriage, Heilbrun bought another house, all for herself. She wanted a house, she said, away from the "family togetherness" of the other house—"small, modern, full of machinery that *worked*, and above all habitable in winter, so that I might sit in front of a fire and contemplate, meditate, conjure, and, if in need of distraction, read."

Then there was Heilbrun's most problematic notion, the one she believed was everyone's moral right: a death of one's own—suicide. The days leading up to hers, at 77, were perfectly ordinary. There was reading, and writing, and endless reorganizing of the apartment with her husband, a retired urban-economics professor and author. Not many people came by the apartment: Heilbrun did not like dinner parties and, despite the fact that she was once a generous hostess, announced late in life that she would no longer give any of her own. Her clothes came from catalogues and dressmakers, and groceries from orders called in to the supermarket. "My mother was a busy woman," says her son, Robert, "and she was not going to waste her time squeezing fruit at Fairway."

Heilbrun spent most of her time with her vast library of modern British literature, mysteries, feminist theory, and works by Woolf. She broke her days up with long walks in Central Park, a cure she took nearly every day for as many years as anyone can remember. When her children were young, she would lure them along with the promise of buying a novel at the old Doubleday [bookstore] on Fifth Avenue. At night, they gathered around her on the couch, delighting in Winnie-the-Pooh, Norse myths, and the Mary Poppins series, all read in Heilbrun's proclamatory yet oddly soothing voice, with just a hint of an English accent.

Tuesday at 11:30 was the time Heilbrun walked in the park with her old friend and colleague Mary Ann Caws, a literary critic and art historian. They had met for walks every week for 26 years, most recently on the corner of 81st Street and Central Park West. They walked their standard route: by Tavern on the Green, curving around to Central Park South, then uptown on the East Side, dodging horse-drawn buggies and in-line skaters and laughably fanatical runners. To all the world they looked like a pair of hausfraus [housewives] chatting about grandchildren—Caws with her gray-blonde bob, Heilbrun in a blouse and slacks (she had stopped wearing nylons and heels at 62, as always, as a matter of principle). In fact, they were discussing [evolutionist Charles] Darwin, [painter Edouard] Manet's *Gare Saint-Lazare*, women's poetry, and the state of the world today, which they deplored.

"I feel sad," Heilbrun said at one point.

"About what?" asked Caws.

"The universe," said Heilbrun.

As always, Heilbrun greeted all oncoming dogs. ("Whether animals admit it or not, they and I communicate," she once wrote.) She would hold out a hand for them to smell. Caws chatted with an owner about her Mephisto flats: They both had pairs. "Well, if you're going to talk about shoes," said Heilbrun, beckoning her away.

After their walk, Heilbrun returned to the apartment, to her reading, her e-mailing, her long talks with colleagues. By all accounts, she did not have an argument with anyone, nor did she contact any long-lost friends. But soon she was found dead, a plastic bag over her head. A note lay nearby: "The journey is over. Love to all."

Suicide Can Be an Act of Choice

At the time of her suicide, Heilbrun was not sick, nor had she been, to anyone's knowledge, recently informed of some impending illness. She had no history of mental illness, nor was she on medication, nor had she been diagnosed as depressed—but then again, Heilbrun did not see a therapist, viewing Freudianism [the thought of psychoanalyst Sigmund Freud] (which she saw as the root of all psychological practice) as inherently anti-woman. "The Freudian view that accomplished women are sexually men, or trying to be, has done more, I suspect, than any other misconception to doom women to fear of accomplishment and selfhood," she once wrote.

Heilbrun's suicide was an act of will, an idea brought to life. It was something she chose, by herself, for herself. And, like everyone in Heilbrun's life, including her children and her husband, Caws was stunned. She sits at Eli's Restaurant, on the Upper East Side, with a cup of coffee. Like Heilbrun, Caws has the acerbic, no-nonsense tone of decades-long professorship but a warm, generous laugh, and an even kinder smile. "You know, Carolyn would ask me at the end of every walk, 'Will you be here next Tuesday?'" she says. "And I can't remember for sure, but last time, I don't think she did ask."

There was a sense, however, in which Heilbrun's death wasn't a complete surprise. In both her writings and in conversation, Heilbrun had often mused about killing herself at 70, which the Bible suggests is the appropriate life span for a human being (not that, as an agnostic, she much cared what the Bible had to say.)

Part of the reason is easy to understand—"To watch parents go on and on and on, and well beyond where they would have liked to have gone, makes one feel strongly that you want to end it while you still are capable of doing so," says Joan Ferrante, a Columbia University professor and friend. "We had agreed for a long time that [suicide] was the sensible way to face things."

And Heilbrun was nothing if not sensible: She made what she considered informed decisions, and seldom second-guessed herself. She disliked idle chitchat, so, at 50, she took a Maoist [Mao Zedong's version of communism] approach to her social life, ordaining that her meetings with friends should be almost wholly restricted to one-on-one affairs. Her dealings with her children, when they were young, were similarly formatted—all were under warning that they would be disowned if they took up smoking or went into advertising, and at camp, all received the long, nearly daily letter from "Mommie" copied on carbon paper. In their teens, they were each suddenly required to cook dinner for the family once a week—it works out perfectly, Heilbrun told friends, as long as you're willing to eat peanut butter and jelly from time to time.

Heilbrun Took Risks in Work and Life

The kinds of choices Heilbrun made in her personal life were natural extensions of the risks she took in her work. As author of a series of a half-dozen books geared to a lay audience (including *Writing a Woman's Life, Reinventing Womanhood, and The Last Gift of Time: Life Beyond Sixty*), onetime president of the Modern Language Association, and occupant of an endowed chair in the English department at Columbia—at least until 1992, when she resigned in protest over what she saw as the department's sexual discrimination—Heilbrun was instrumental in securing a place for both female characters and female writers in the serious study of literature. She argued for the importance of the uniquely female experience of reading in clear, candid language: "Women, I believe, search for fellow beings who have faced similar struggles, conveyed them in ways a reader can transform into her own life, confirmed desires the reader had hardly acknowledged—desires that now seem possible. Women catch courage from the women whose lives and writings they read, and women call the bearer of that courage friend."

It is this courage to choose—to live life as you want, and to hell with everyone else, even those who love you—that both enriched Heilbrun's life, and hastened her death. [Novelist] E.M. Forster writes, "It is difficult, after accepting six cups of tea, to throw the seventh in the face of your hostess," but Heilbrun made a life of, as she writes, "flinging the conventional tea," whether it was accepting [poet] Adrienne Rich's notion that women could express their true feelings about their children, or committing suicide, an act considered sinful since the age of Augustine [an influential fifth-century Catholic theologian]. For Heilbrun, old age was a time of what she calls "borrowed time": "Each day one can say to oneself: I can always die; do I choose death or life? I daily choose life the more earnestly because it is a choice," she wrote.

Not being able to make choices meant becoming what Heilbrun called a "useless person." "Carol had a strong ethical sense, about as strong as anyone I've ever known," says Heilbrun's oldest friend, Tom F. Driver, a retired professor at Union Theological Seminary, down the hill from Columbia's campus. "It was her intention to live a moral life, and one of the components of that life was that life ought to be *for* something."

Death, on the other hand, she invested with no meaning at all. She left no instructions for her memorial, or about what to do with her body: Her family knew only that she had once commented, after the death of the family cat, that she didn't have any feelings on that topic. "You can flush my ashes down the toilet, for all I care," she said.

The most important part of any story is, nevertheless, its ending. For women, the plot has famously concluded in marriage or death, real or symbolic, either by one's own hand or another's. Suicide can be an escape hatch from the patriarchal structure, as in the long swim of the protagonist in Kate Chopin's *The Awakening*, or for that matter, [in the 1991 film] *Thelma and Louise*, and there is a history of it among prominent modern women writers, from Woolf (rocks in the pockets, walks into lake) to poet Anne Sexton (carbon-monoxide poisoning in garage) to Sylvia Plath (head in oven). Heilbrun's friends answer questions about the connection between these women's deaths and Heilbrun's cautiously; they do not want a link made. "This is a person who was inventive and energetic and gutsy, and that same person at some point decided to stop living," says Judith Resnik, Yale Law professor, co-author, and friend. "This is not part of an ideology of feminism—this was a person who made her own decisions, as her own person." . . .

Suicide Was Part of Heilbrun's Feminism

Sometimes Heilbrun saw promise in getting older. She wrote, "Neither rocking on a porch, nor automatically offering her services as cook and housekeeper and child watcher, nor awaiting another chapter in the heterosexual plot, the old woman must be glimpsed through all her disguises which seem to preclude her right to be called woman. She may well for the first time be woman herself."

But there were also pitfalls to age: stasis, puttering, becoming a "useless person," sinking "into the ancient sin of anomie when challenges failed." To be inconsequential, for Heilbrun, was to die. She had said so much about women, their lives, and writing; she wanted to focus on something else. She turned in the last few years to the biographies of scientists, taking solace in the fact that science had tests, and answers. She did not understand their theories—"my comprehension is best expounded by [the first president of the State of Israel] Chaim Weizmann, describing a transatlantic crossing with [physicist Albert] Einstein: 'Einstein explained his theory to me every day; by the time we arrived, I was finally convinced that he understood it.'"

For someone in the throes of this kind of creative crossroads, suicide can have a distinct appeal. So is that how hers should be read? As always, the textual evidence is conflicting. On one hand, Heilbrun was clearly casting about for something new to do. She writes, "Here is [Gerard Manley] Hopkins, perfectly conveying what is these days my chief despair: 'Birds build—but not I build; no, but strain, Time's eunuch, and not breed one work that wakes. Mine, O thou Lord of life, send my roots rain.'"

On the other hand, Heilbrun's suicide was part of the plan she had all along, perhaps an essential component of her feminism. She writes, "We women have lived too much with closure—there always seems to loom the possibility of something being over, settled, sweeping clear the way for contentment. This is the delusion of a passive life. When the hope for closure is abandoned, when there is an end to fantasy, adventure for women will begin. Endings—the kind [Jane] Austen tacked onto her novels—are for romance or daydreams, but not for life."

And suicide, while on one level is closure, is a kind of freedom on another. "The thing about suicide is that it is indeterminate," says Susan Gubar, Heilbrun's friend and a professor at Indiana University. "The only person to testify with any authenticity is God. Everyone else is bullshitting."

In Heilbrun's apartment, over the fireplace, there is a self-portrait by Vanessa Bell, Virginia Woolf's sister. The Heilbruns bought the piece over 25 years ago, along with another portrait of Bell's (homosexual) lover, Duncan Grant, at a time when Heilbrun had curly brown hair and, she writes, "was hardly a beauty, while Vanessa Bell's beauty was widely celebrated." In the painting, however, Bell appears in a serious pose, wearing glasses, her gray hair fastened in a bun. As the years passed, Heilbrun took to wearing her long gray hair pulled back in a bun as well, and she began to resemble, if not Bell, then the portrait, at first faintly and then strongly. She took pleasure in this.

For Further Discussion

1. In *The Awakening*, Kate Chopin describes an unconventional marriage, a theme that recurs in her fiction. What are some aspects of her personal history, as related by the authors in chapter 1, that might cause her to be interested in this theme?

2. In chapter 2 Peggy Skaggs states that none of the three major female characters in *The Awakening*—Edna Pontellier, Adèle Ratignolle, and Mademoiselle Reisz—achieves her full potential as a human being. What aspects of the feminine character does each represent? In your opinion, who comes closest to authenticity? Who do you find most sympathetic?

3. In chapter 2 Elizabeth Fox-Genovese finds *The Awakening* to be concerned with personal rather than social issues. What reasons does she give to support her position? Do you agree with her? Why or why not?

4. Many critics consider the ending of *The Awakening* to be ambivalent. In chapter 2 Per Seyersted argues that Edna asserts her freedom through her suicide, while Barbara C. Ewell contends that Edna ultimately fails to achieve selfhood. Do you think *The Awakening* is an optimistic or pessimistic novel? Why?

5. In chapter 3 Jessica Valenti writes that, while it has become out of fashion for young women to consider themselves feminists, feminism is still very relevant for young women. What reasons does she give to support her position? Do you agree with her? Explain.

For Further Reading

Kate Chopin, *Bayou Folk*. Boston: Houghton Mifflin, 1894.

Michael Cunningham, *The Hours*. New York: Farrar, Straus & Giroux, 1998.

Theodore Dreiser, *Sister Carrie*. New York: Doubleday, 1900.

Jeffrey Eugenides, *The Virgin Suicides*. New York: Farrar, Straus & Giroux, 1993.

Gustave Flaubert, *Madame Bovary: A Tale of Provincial Life*. Philadelphia: T.B. Peterson, 1881.

Charlotte Perkins Gilman, *Herland*. New York: Pantheon, 1979.

———, *The Yellow Wallpaper*. Boston: Small Maynard, 1899.

Nathaniel Hawthorne, *The Scarlet Letter: A Romance*. Boston: Ticknor, Reed, and Fields, 1850.

Rosie Thomas, *The White Dove*. New York: Viking, 1986.

Edith Wharton, *The House of Mirth*. New York: Scribner's, 1905.

Tennessee Williams, *A Streetcar Named Desire*. New York: New Directions, 1947.

Virginia Woolf, *Mrs. Dalloway*. New York: Harcourt, Brace, 1925.

Bibliography

Books

Hiroko Arima | *Beyond and Alone! The Theme of Isolation in Selected Short Fiction of Kate Chopin, Katherine Anne Porter, and Eudora Welty.* Lanham, MD: University Press of America, 2006.

Christopher Benfey | *Degas in New Orleans: Encounters in the Creole World of Kate Chopin and George Washington Cable.* Berkeley: University of California Press, 1997.

Lynda S. Boren and Sara deSaussure Davis, eds. | *Kate Chopin Reconsidered: Beyond the Bayou.* Baton Rouge: Louisiana State University Press, 1992.

Carol P. Christ | *Diving Deep and Surfacing: Women Writers on Spiritual Quest.* Boston: Beacon, 1980.

Susan J. Douglas | *Enlightened Feminism: The Seductive Message That Feminism's Work Is Done.* New York: Times Books, 2010.

Kathleen Gerson | *The Unfinished Revolution: How a New Generation Is Reshaping Family, Work, and Gender in America.* New York: Oxford University Press, 2010.

Amber E. Kinser | *Motherhood and Feminism.* Berkeley, CA: Seal Press, 2010.

Wendy Martin, ed.   *New Essays on "The Awakening."* New York: Cambridge University Press, 1988.

Daniel S. Rankin   *Kate Chopin and Her Creole Stories.* Philadelphia: University of Pennsylvania Press, 1932.

Anne Rowe   "Kate Chopin." In *The History of Southern Literature.* Edited by Louis D. Rubin Jr. et al. Baton Rouge: Louisiana State University Press, 1985.

Helen Taylor   *Gender, Race, and Region in the Writings of Grace King, Ruth McEnery Stuart, and Kate Chopin.* Baton Rouge: Louisiana State University Press, 1989.

Emily Toth   *Kate Chopin.* New York: Morrow, 1990.

Periodicals

Maria Anastasopoulou   "Rites of Passage in Kate Chopin's *The Awakening*," *Southern Literary Journal,* vol. 23, no. 2, 1991.

Robert Arner   "Kate Chopin," *Louisiana Studies,* Spring 1975.

Phyllis W. Barrett   "More American Adams: Women Heroes in American Fiction," *Markham Review,* vol. 10, 1981.

Wayne Batten   "Illusion and Archetype: The Curious Story of Edna Pontellier," *Southern Literary Journal*, vol. 18, no. 1, 1985.

Mary M. Bendel-Simso   "Mothers, Women and Creole Mother-Women in Kate Chopin's South," *Southern Studies*, vol. 3, no. 1, 1992.

Ottavio Mark Casale   "Beyond Sex: The Dark Romanticism of Kate Chopin's *The Awakening*," *Ball State University Forum*, vol. 19, no. 1, 1978.

Lloyd M. Daigrepont   "Edna Pontellier and the Myth of Passion," *New Orleans Review*, vol. 18, no. 3, 1991.

Irene Dash   "The Literature of Birth and Abortion." *Regionalism and the Female Imagination*, vol. 3, no. 1, 1977.

Cathy N. Davidson   "Chopin and Atwood: Woman Drowning, Woman Surfacing," *Kate Chopin Newsletter*, vol. 1, no. 3, 1975.

Kenneth Eble   "A Forgotten Novel: Kate Chopin's *The Awakening*," *Western Humanities Review*, Summer 1956.

Marie Fletcher   "The Southern Woman in the Fiction of Kate Chopin," *Louisiana History*, vol. 7, 1966.

Suzanne Disheroon Green, et al.   "Remembering Kate Chopin on the Centennial Anniversary of *The Awakening*," *Southern Studies*, vol. 8, nos. 1–2, 1997.

James H. Justus   "The Unawakening of Edna Pontellier," *Southern Literary Journal*, vol. 10, no. 2, 1978.

Kathleen Margaret Lant   "The Siren of Grand Isle: Adele's Role in *The Awakening*," *Southern Studies*, vol. 23, no. 2, 1984.

Peggy Orenstein   "The Empowerment Mystique," *New York Times Magazine*, September 26, 2010.

Katha Pollit   "Feminist Mothers, Flapper Daughters," *Nation*, October 18, 2010.

Marco Portales   "The Characterization of Edna Pontellier and the Conclusion of Kate Chopin's *The Awakening*," *Southern Studies*, vol. 20, no. 4, 1981.

Hanna Rosin   "The End of Men," *Atlantic Monthly*, July/August 2010.

William Schuyler   "Kate Chopin," *Writer*, August 1894.

Carisa Showden   "What's Political About the New Feminisms?," *Frontiers: A Journal of Women's Studies*, vol. 30, no. 2, 2009.

Christine Stansell   "Global Feminism in a Conservative Age: Possibilities and Pieties Since 1980," *Dissent*, Spring 2010.

Jessica Valenti   "Who Stole Feminism?," *Nation*, October 18, 2010.

Cynthia G. Wolff   "Thanatos and Eros: Kate Chopin's
The Awakening," *American Quarterly*,
October 1973.

Index

Women
changing roles of, 11–13, 66, 67–69, 122–123, 128–137
choices by, 148–149, 152
communication by, on Internet, 168–173
condition of, 117–118
in Creole society, 92–94
desire for children by, 91–92
freedom for, 106–108
independent, 60–64, 69, 125–126
inequality of, 81–85
key to happiness for, 152–156
lack of control of, 31–32
lack of voice for, 95–96
in Louisiana, 71–72
love between, 38–39
male ego and, 113–115
middle-class, 124
mother-women, 81, 101, 107, 134–135
northern, 124
objectification of, by marriage, 119–122
objectification of, by popular culture, 141–143
overly passionate, 77–78
in popular culture, 141–143
powerlessness of, 144–145
selfhood for, 97–103, 118–119
southern, 12, 121–127
in workforce, 12, 66
See also Female sexuality
Women and Economics (Gilman), 67
Women writers
in nineteenth century, 69
suicides by, 180
Women's clubs, 12, 14
Women's rights movement, 12, 35, 71, 121–122, 125
Woodhull, Victoria Claflin, 14
Woolf, Virginia, 113, 174, 175, 180
Workforce, women in, 12, 66
Wright, Wendy, 162–163

Y

The Yellow Wallpaper (Gilman), 96, 118, 120
Young Dr. Gosse (Chopin), 26, 27, 54

Z

Ziff, Larzer, 67, 69, 112, 116
Zola, Émile, 30, 54–56

CPSIA information can be obtained
at www.ICGtesting.com
Printed in the USA
FFOW02n1843130614
5907FF

9 780737 758207